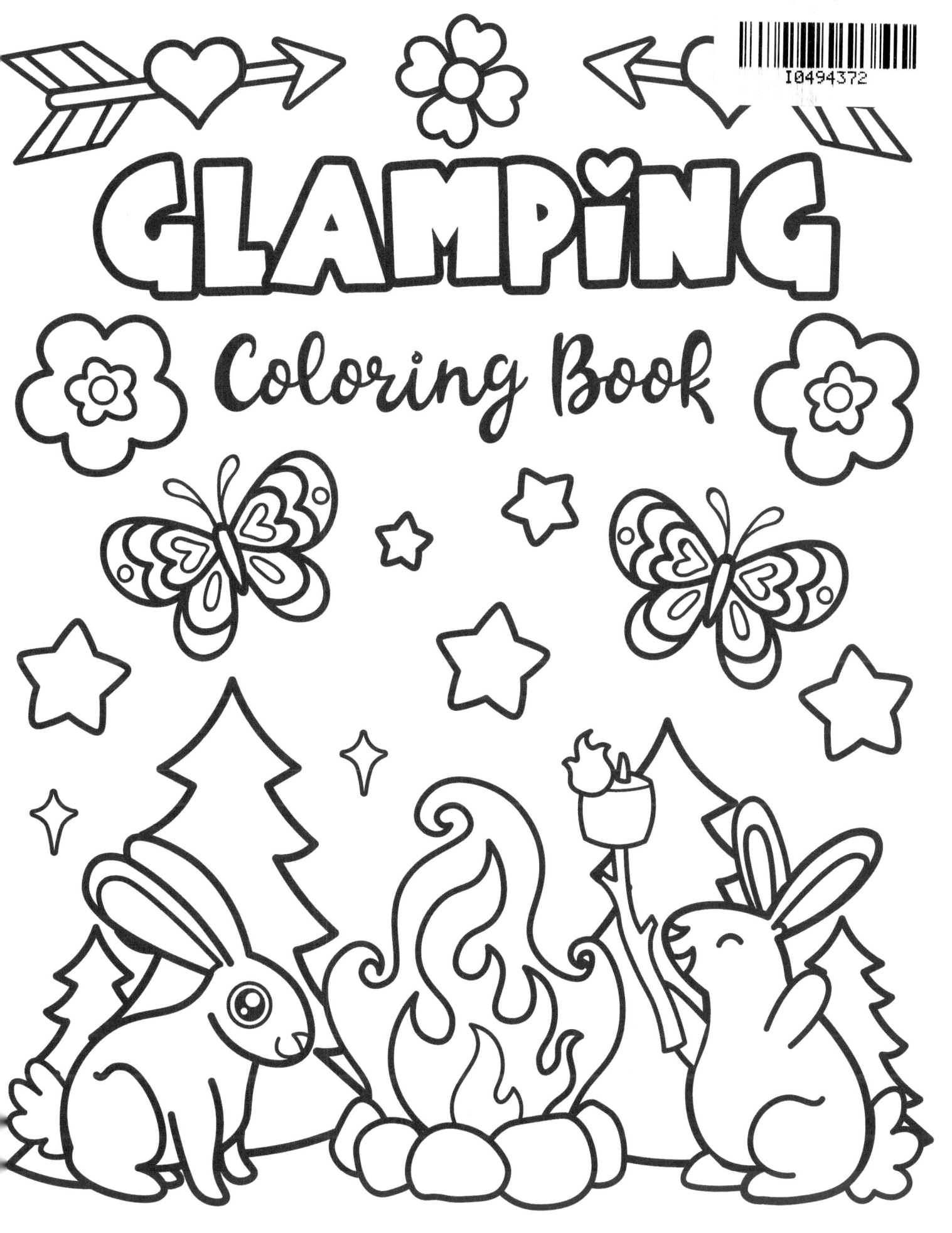

GLAMPiNG

Coloring Book

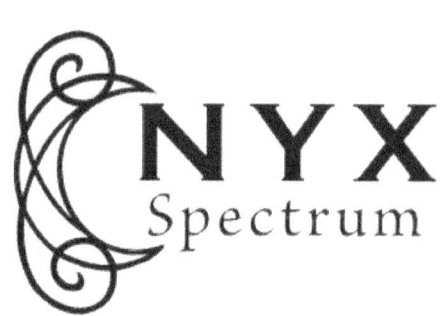

Published in 2019 by
Nyx Spectrum

Printed in the United States of America

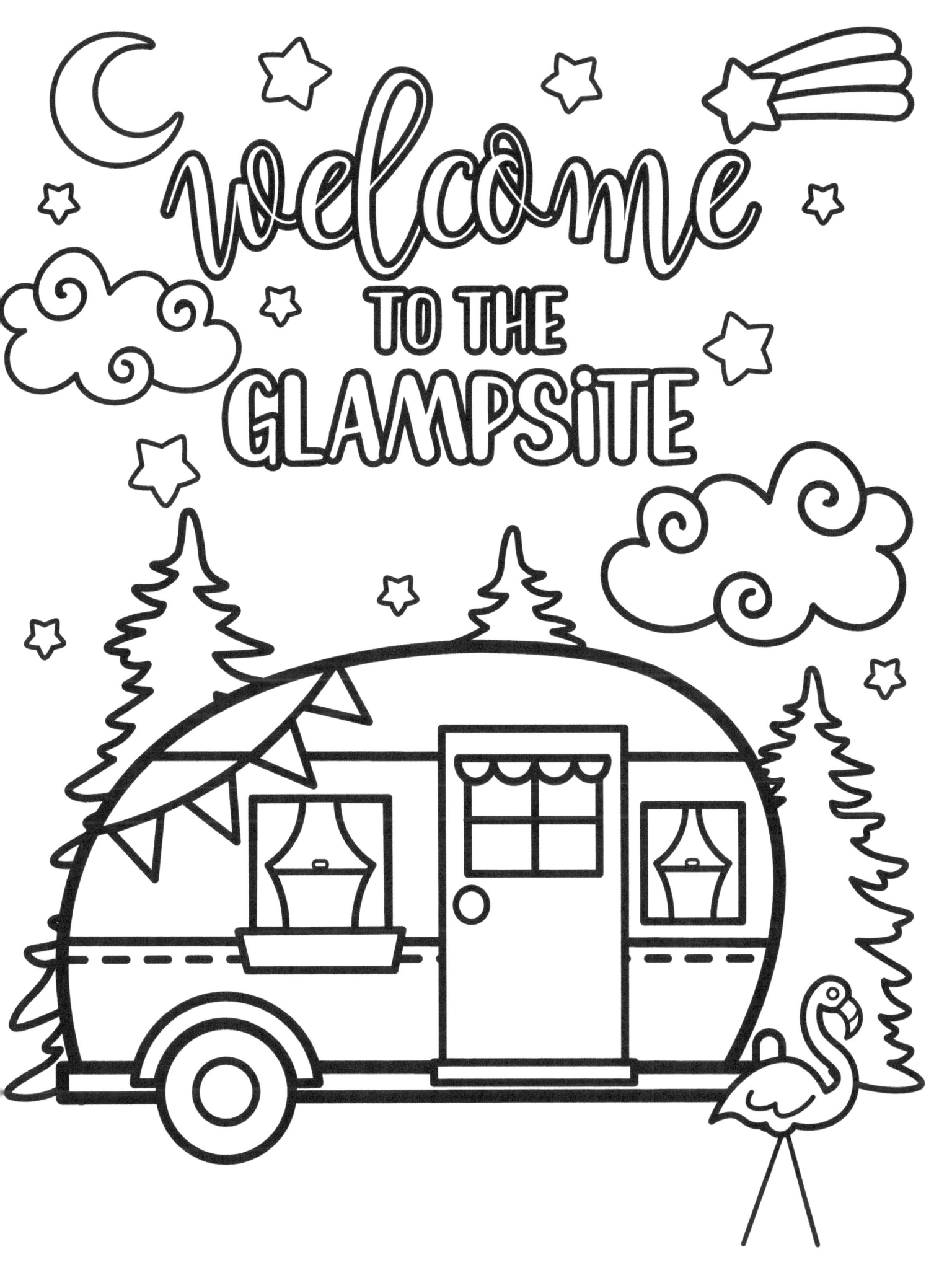

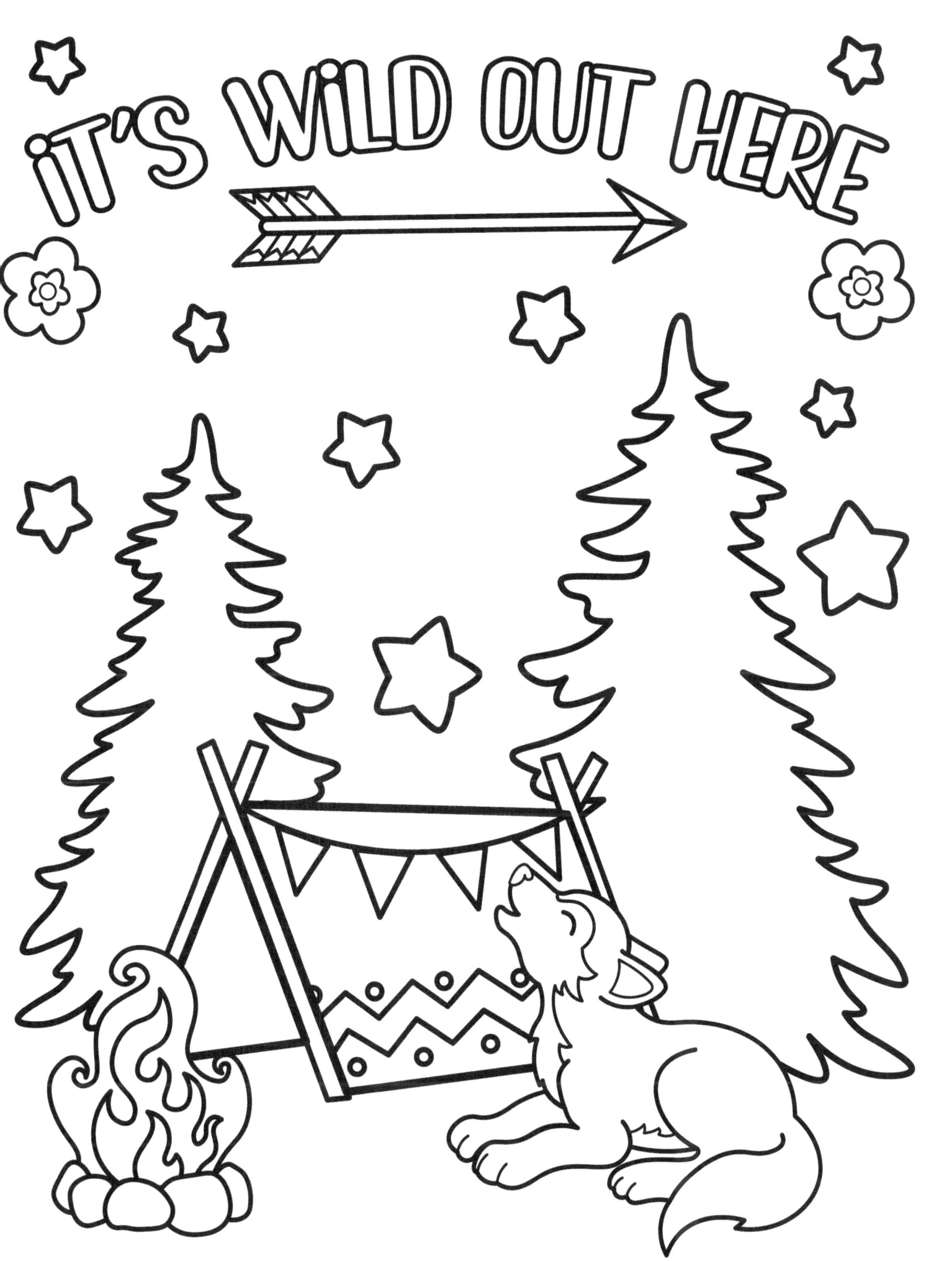

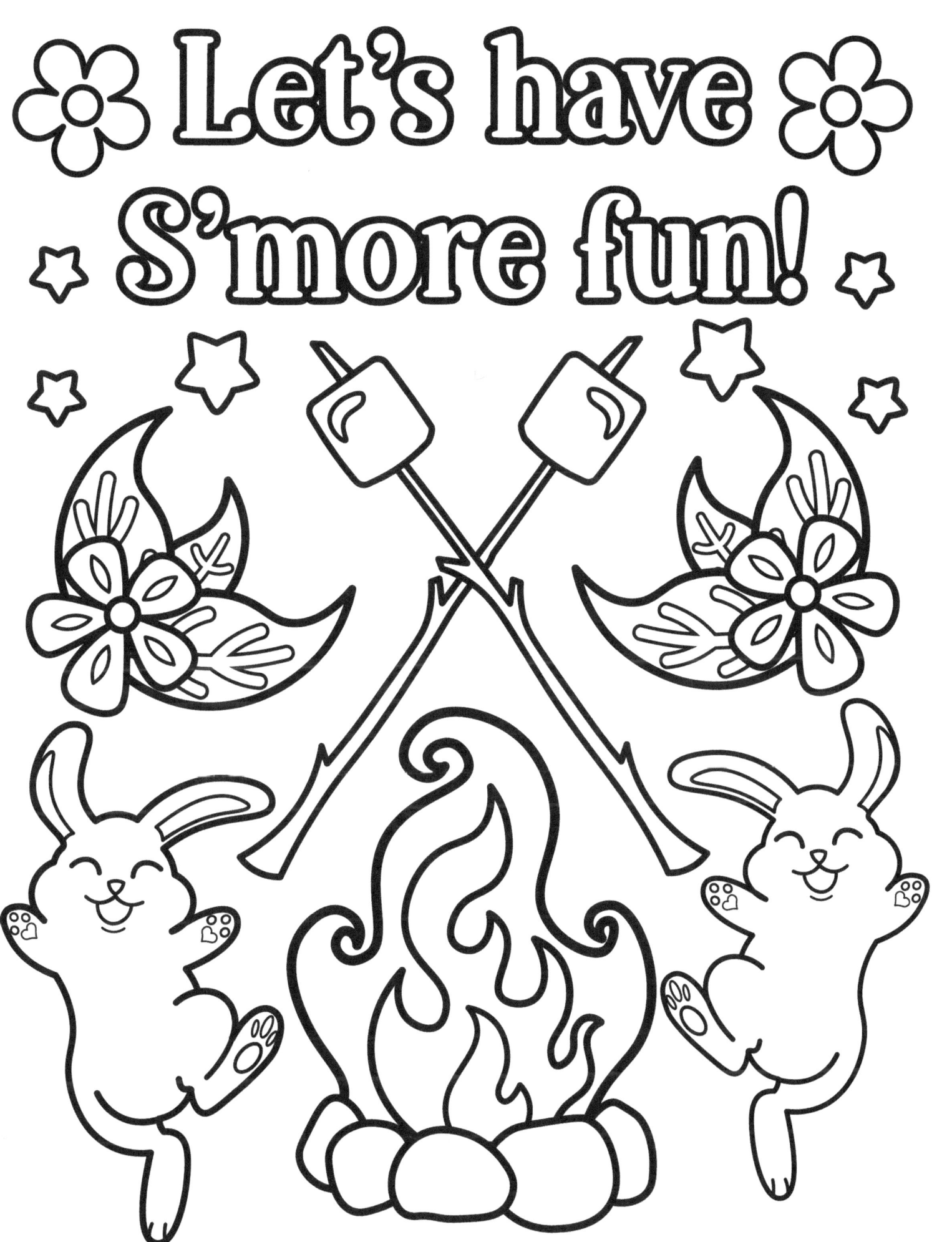

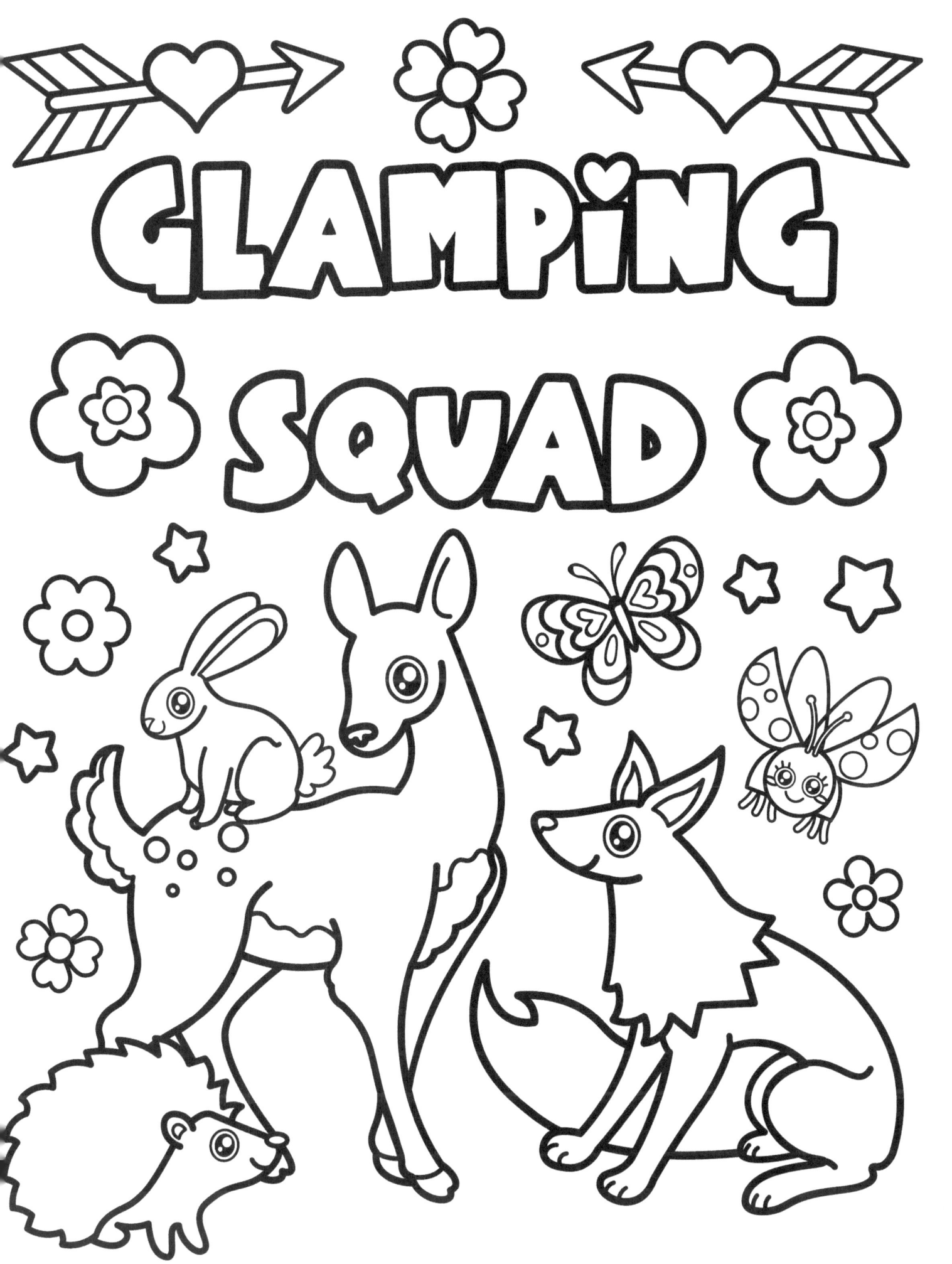

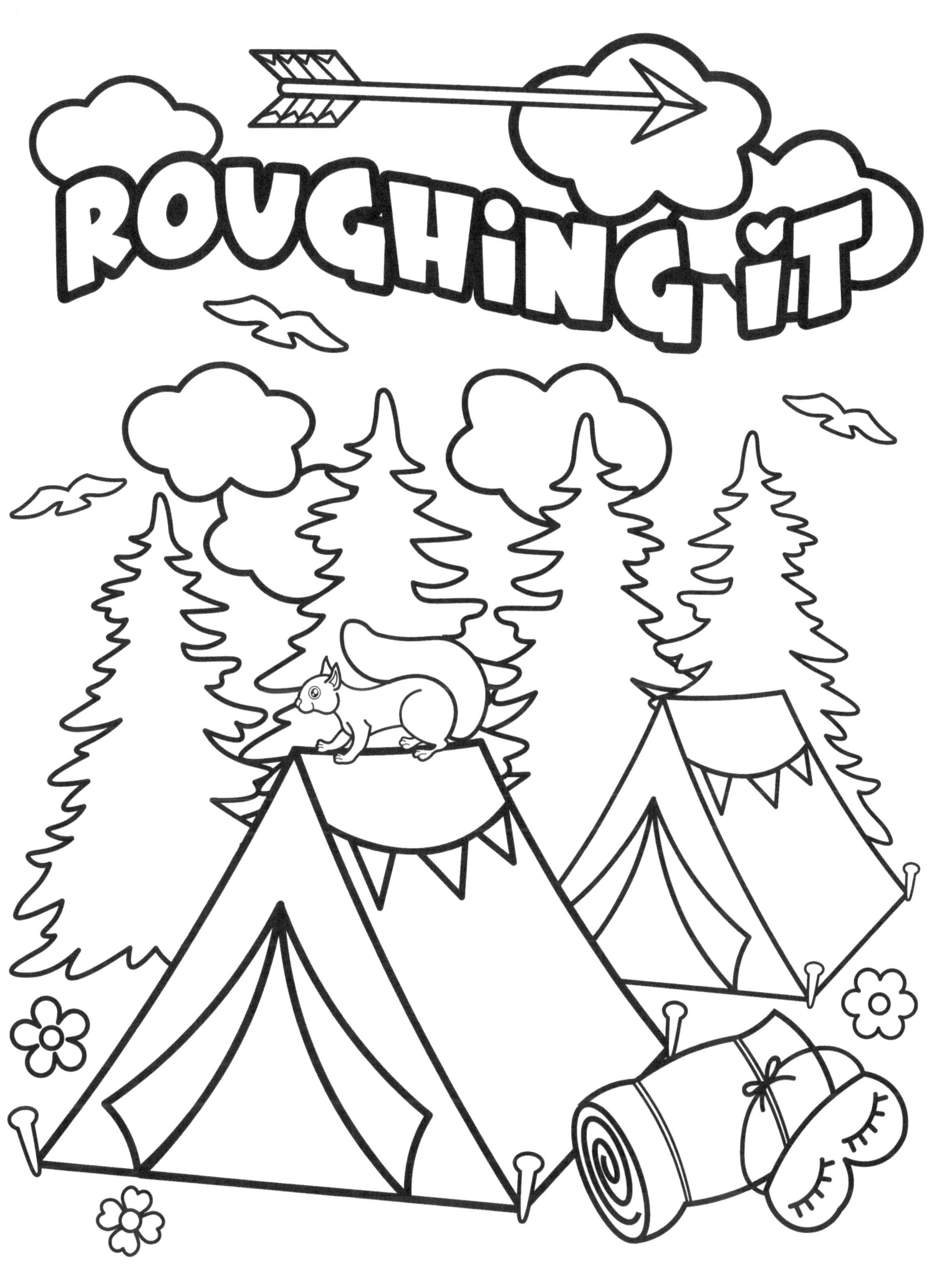

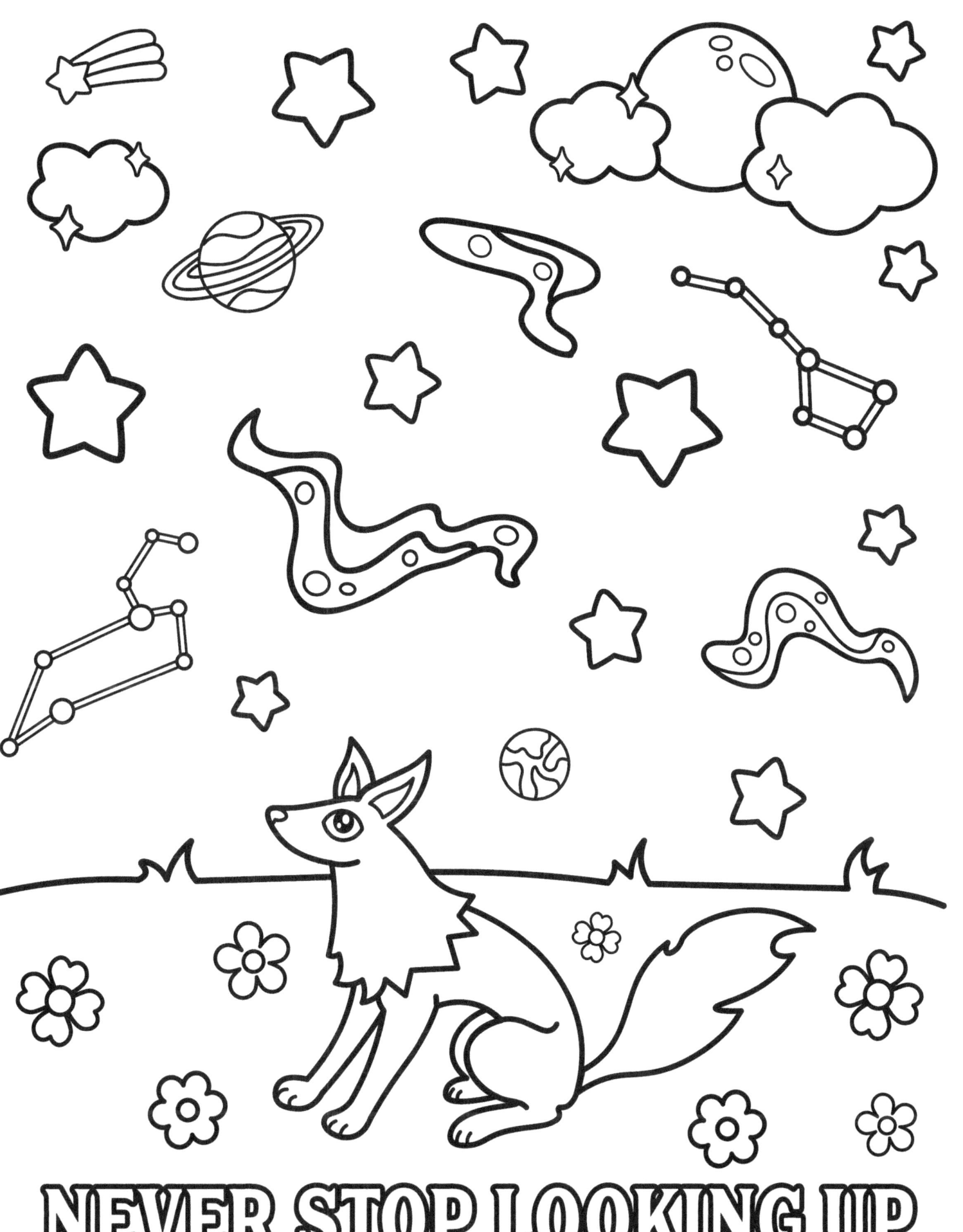

NEVER STOP LOOKING UP

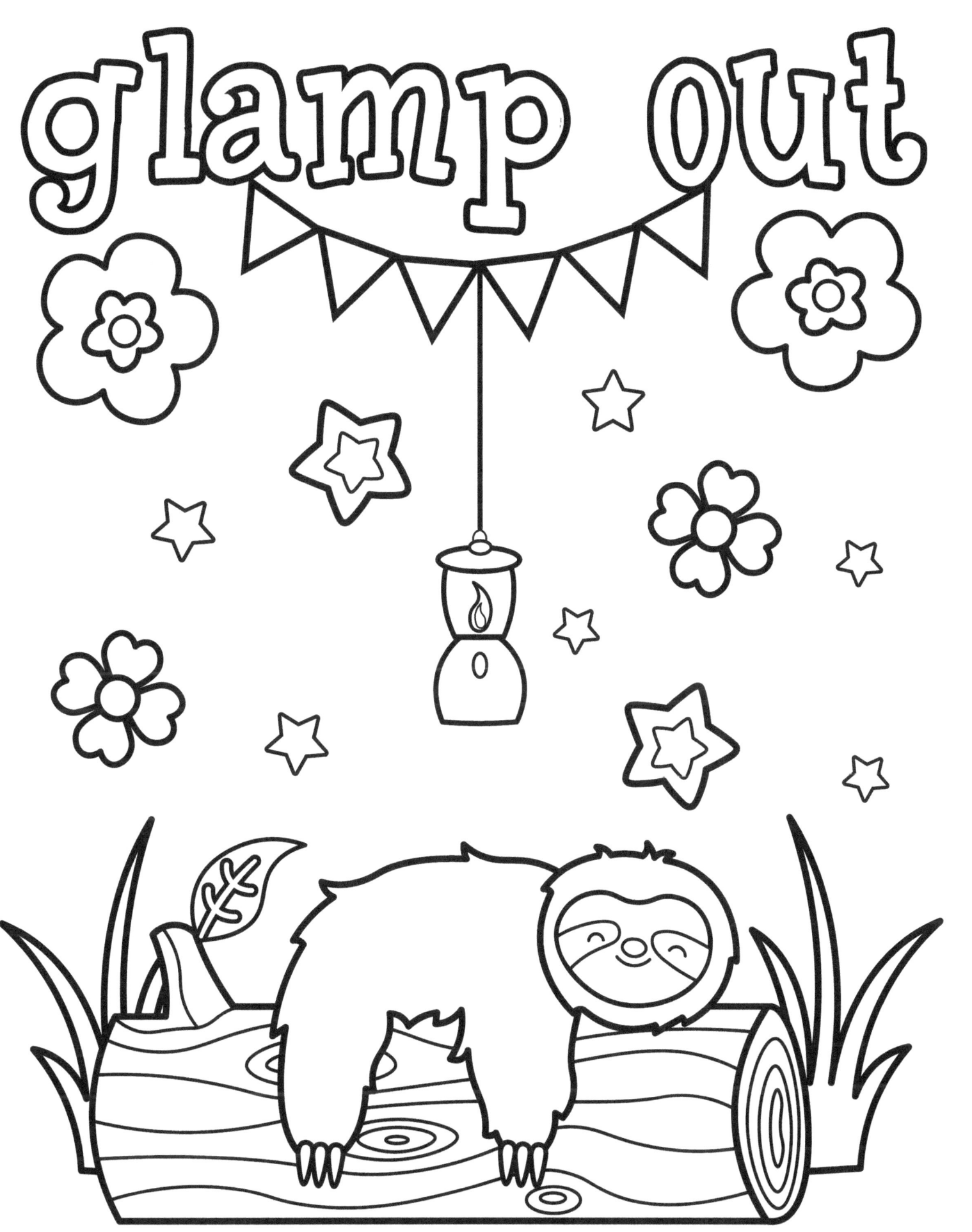

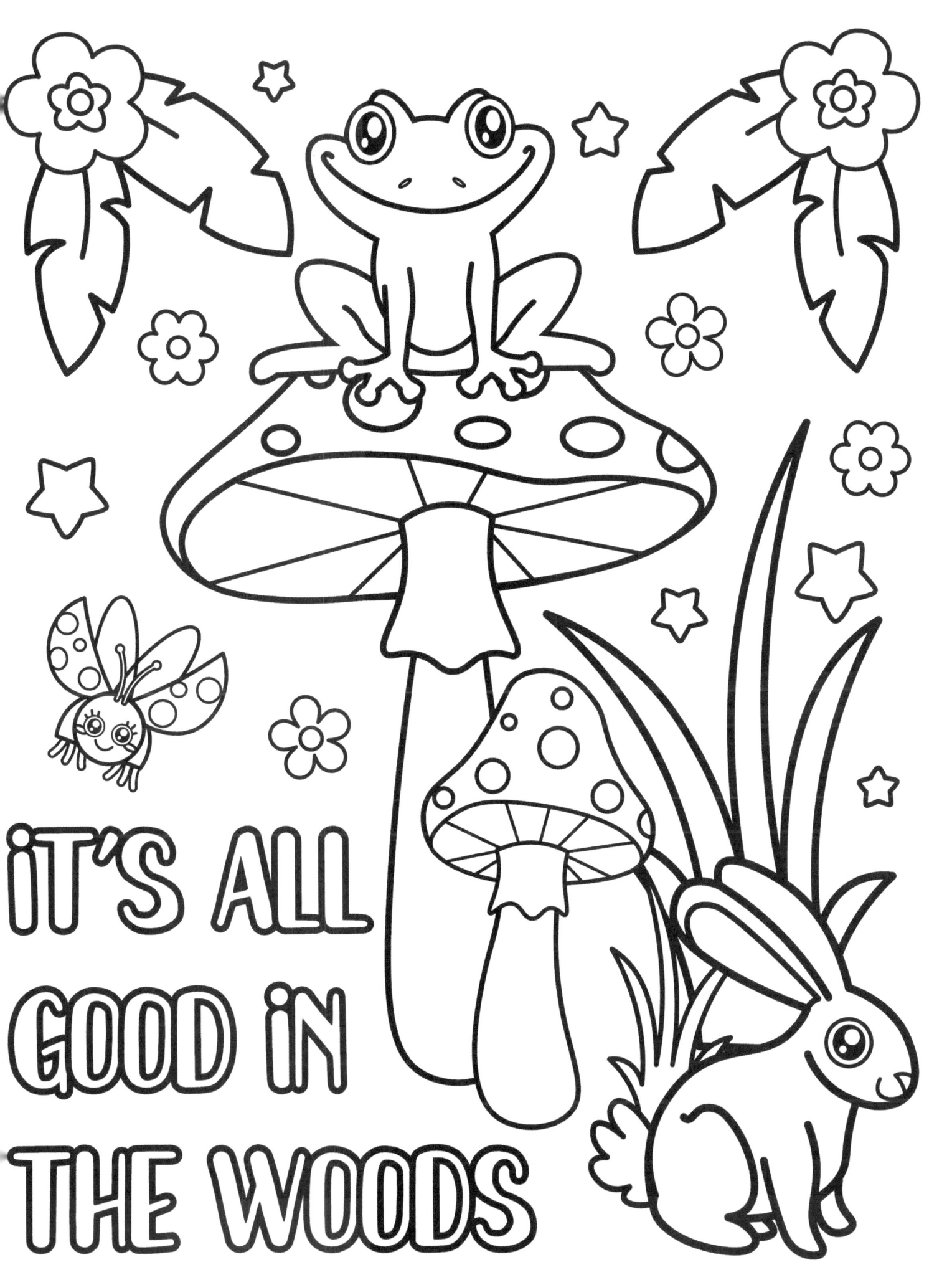

IT'S ALL GOOD IN THE WOODS

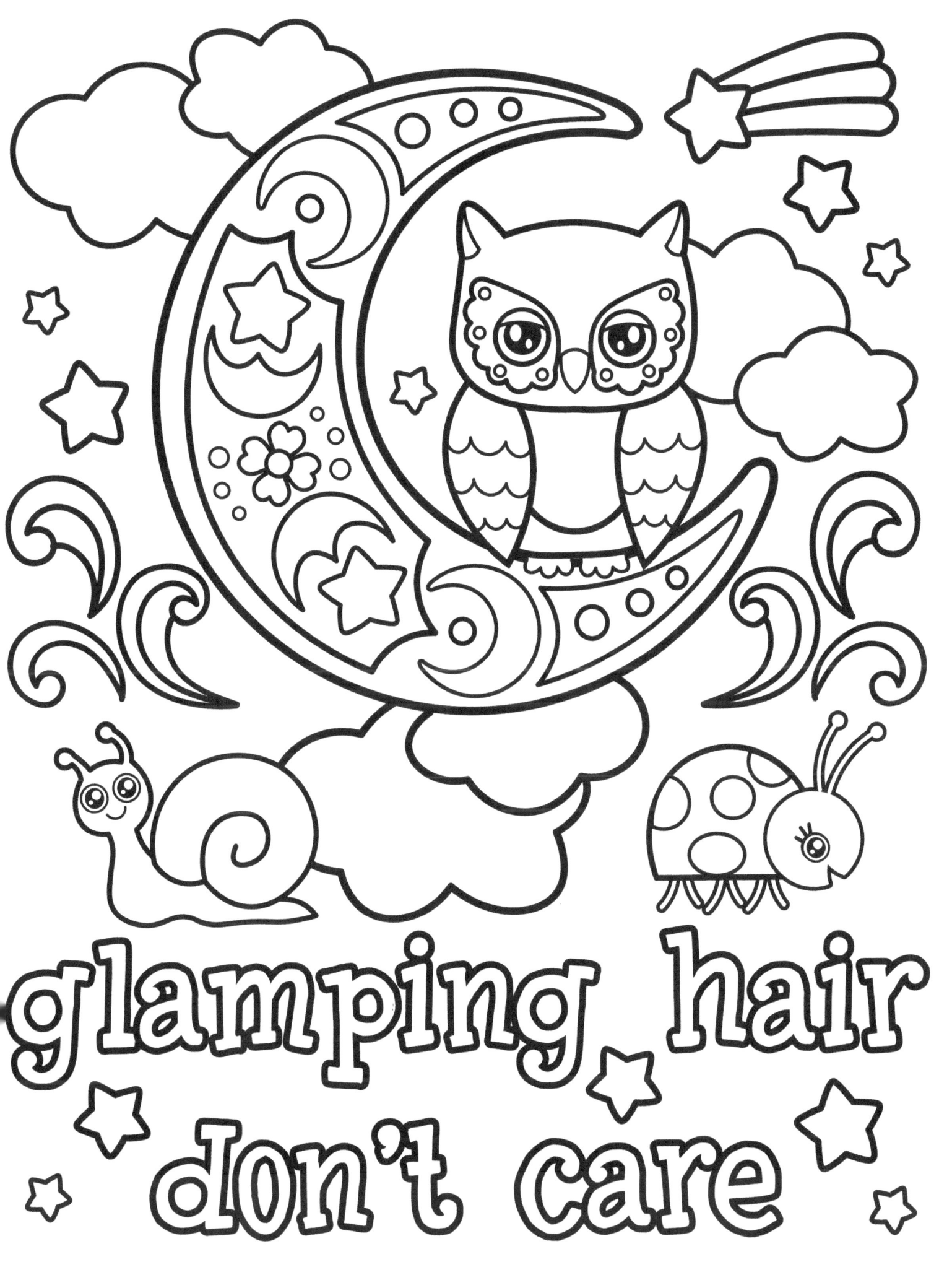

glamping hair
don't care

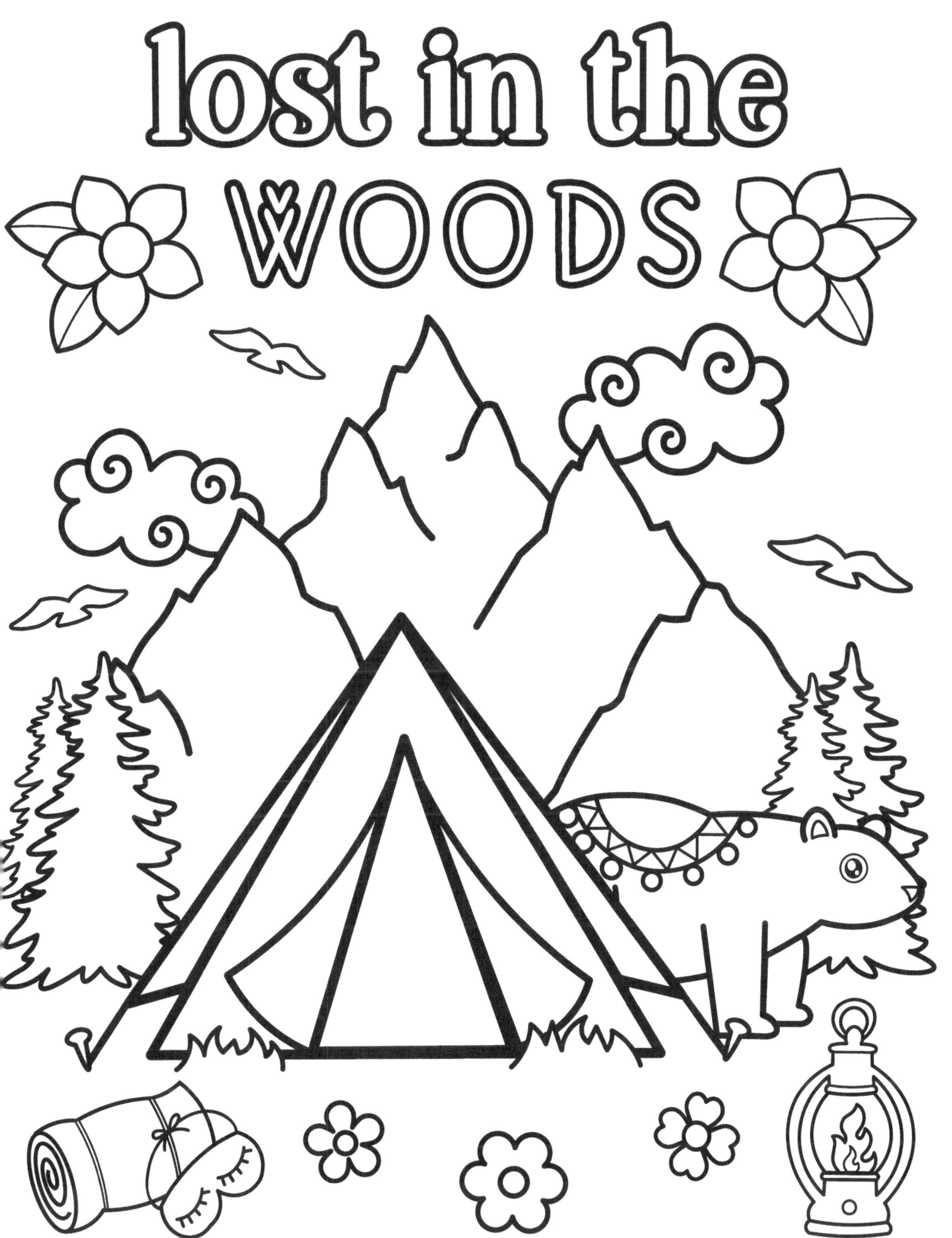

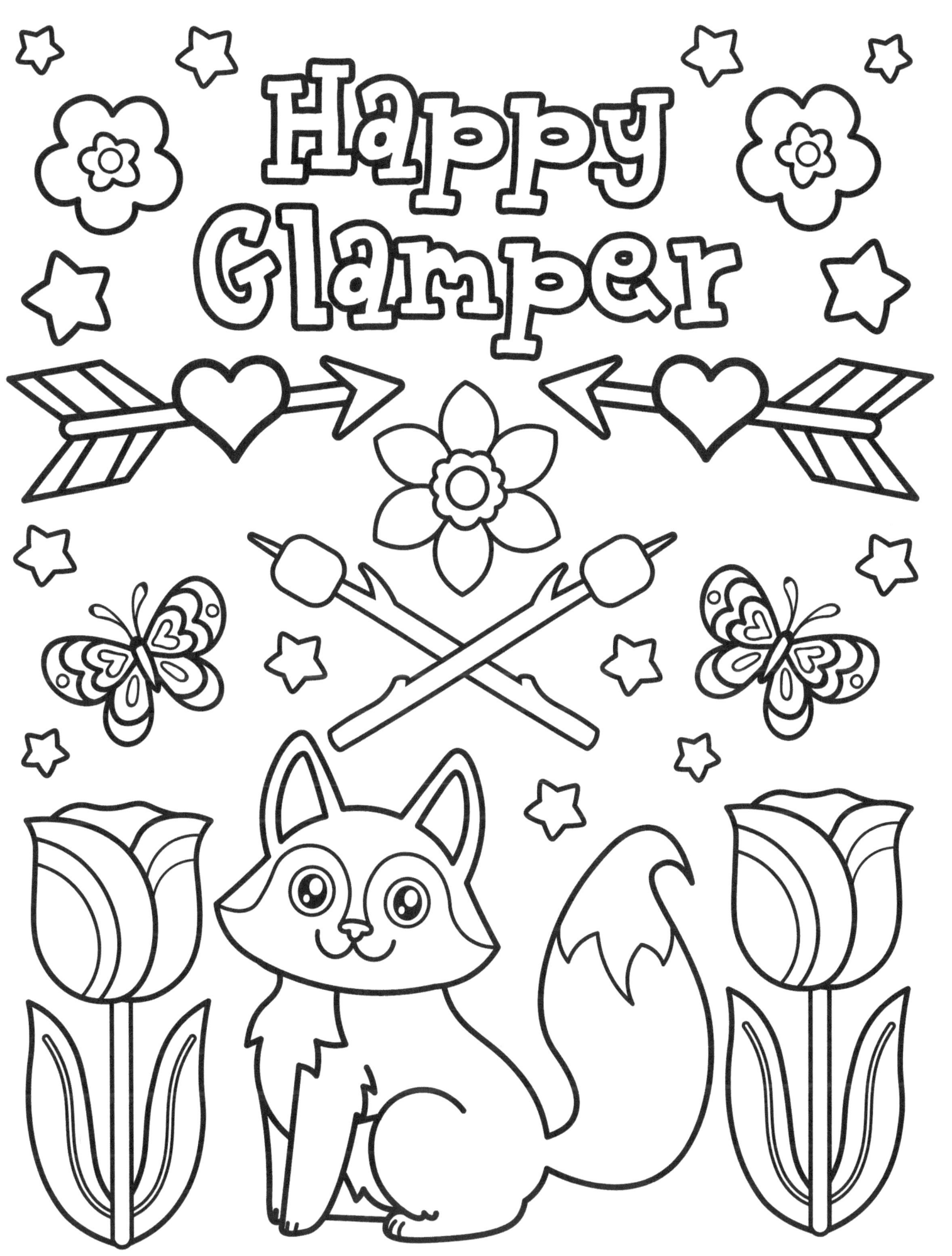

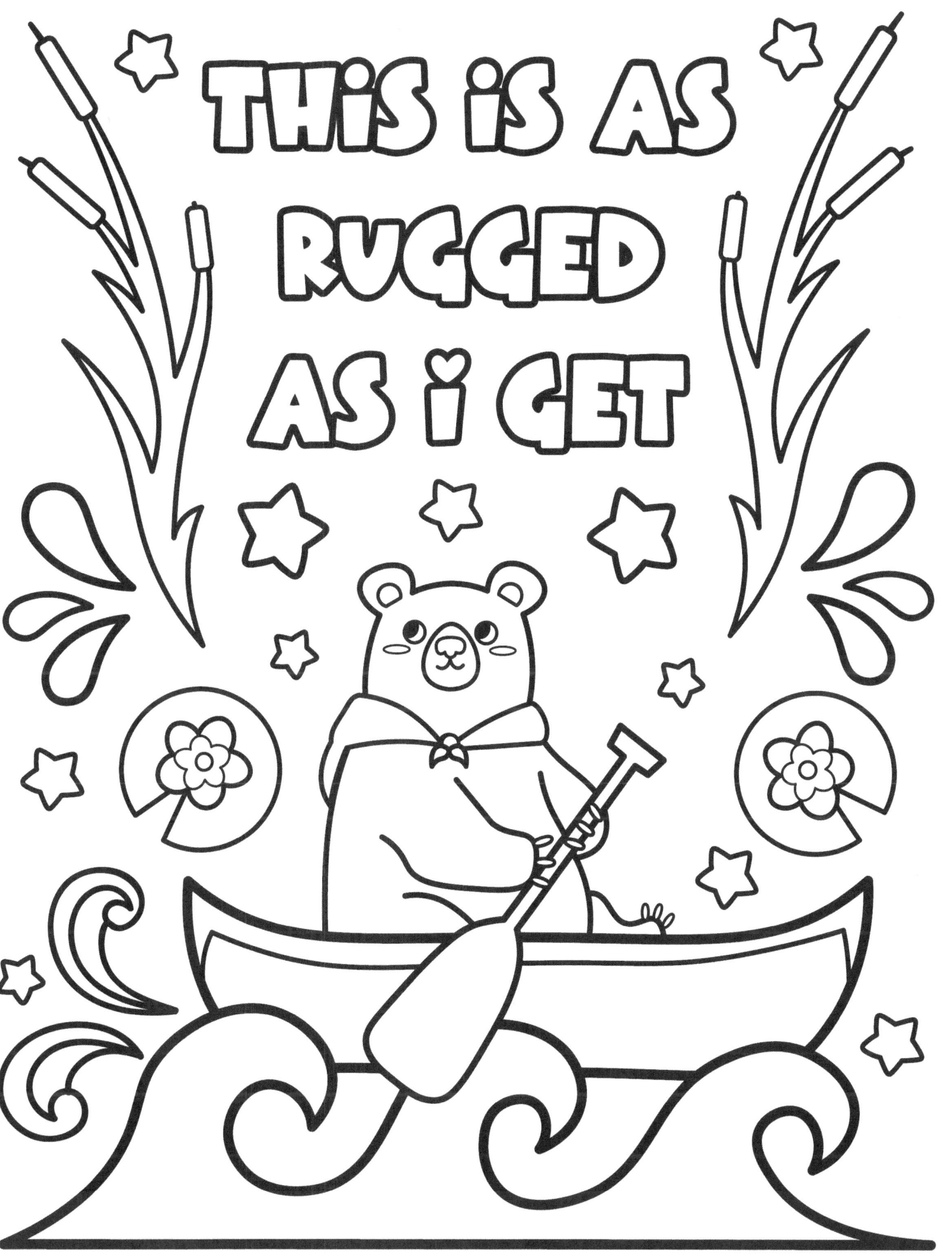

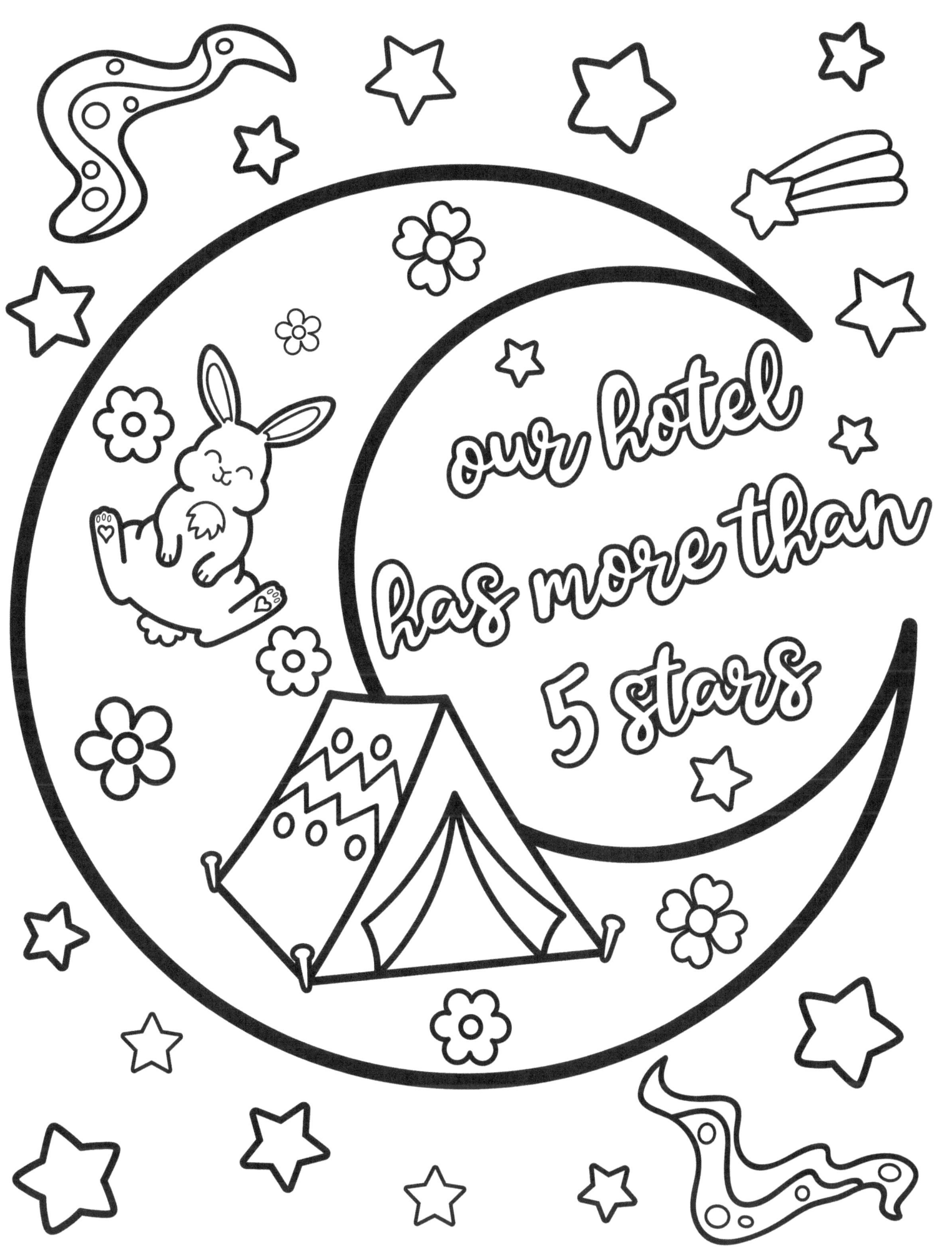

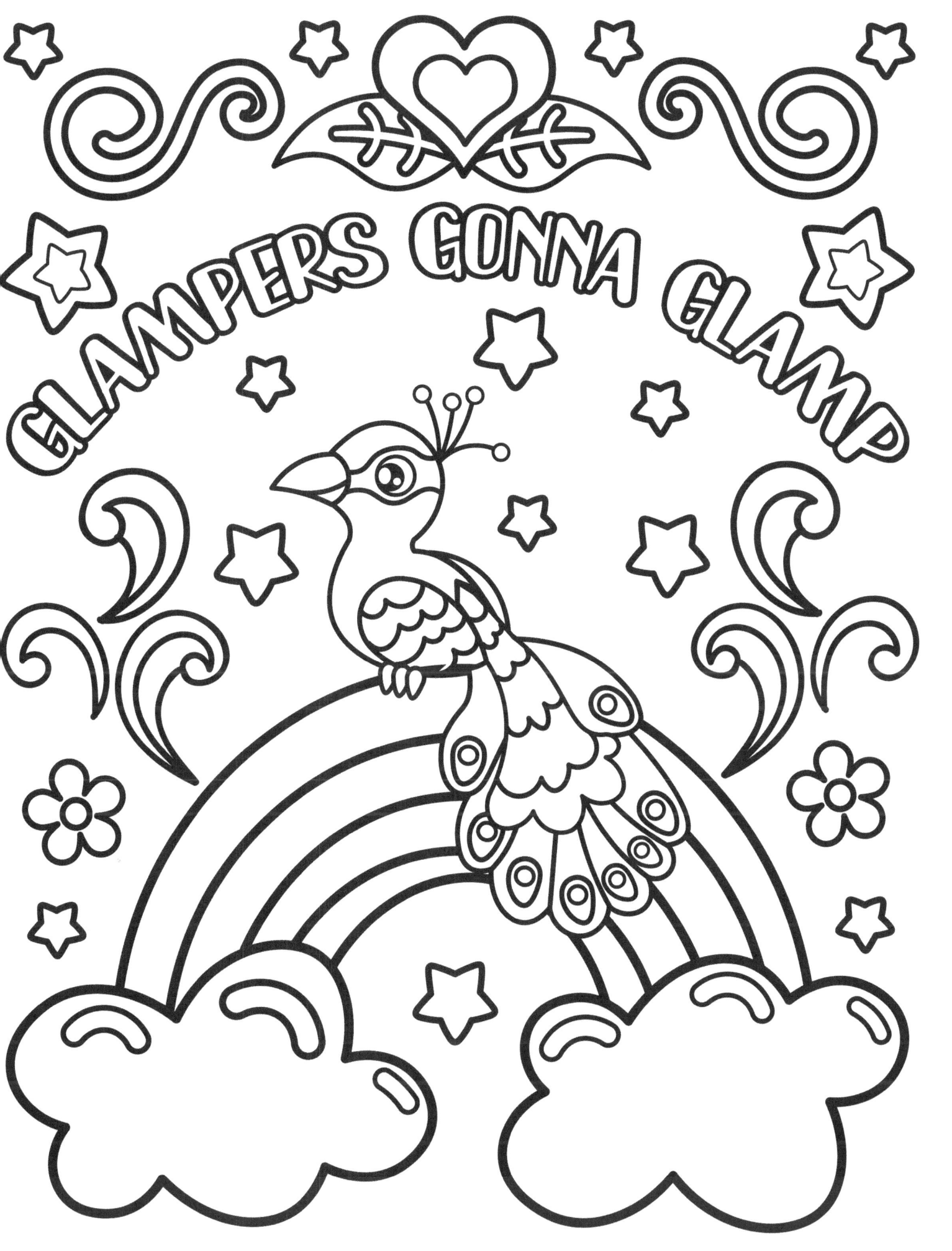

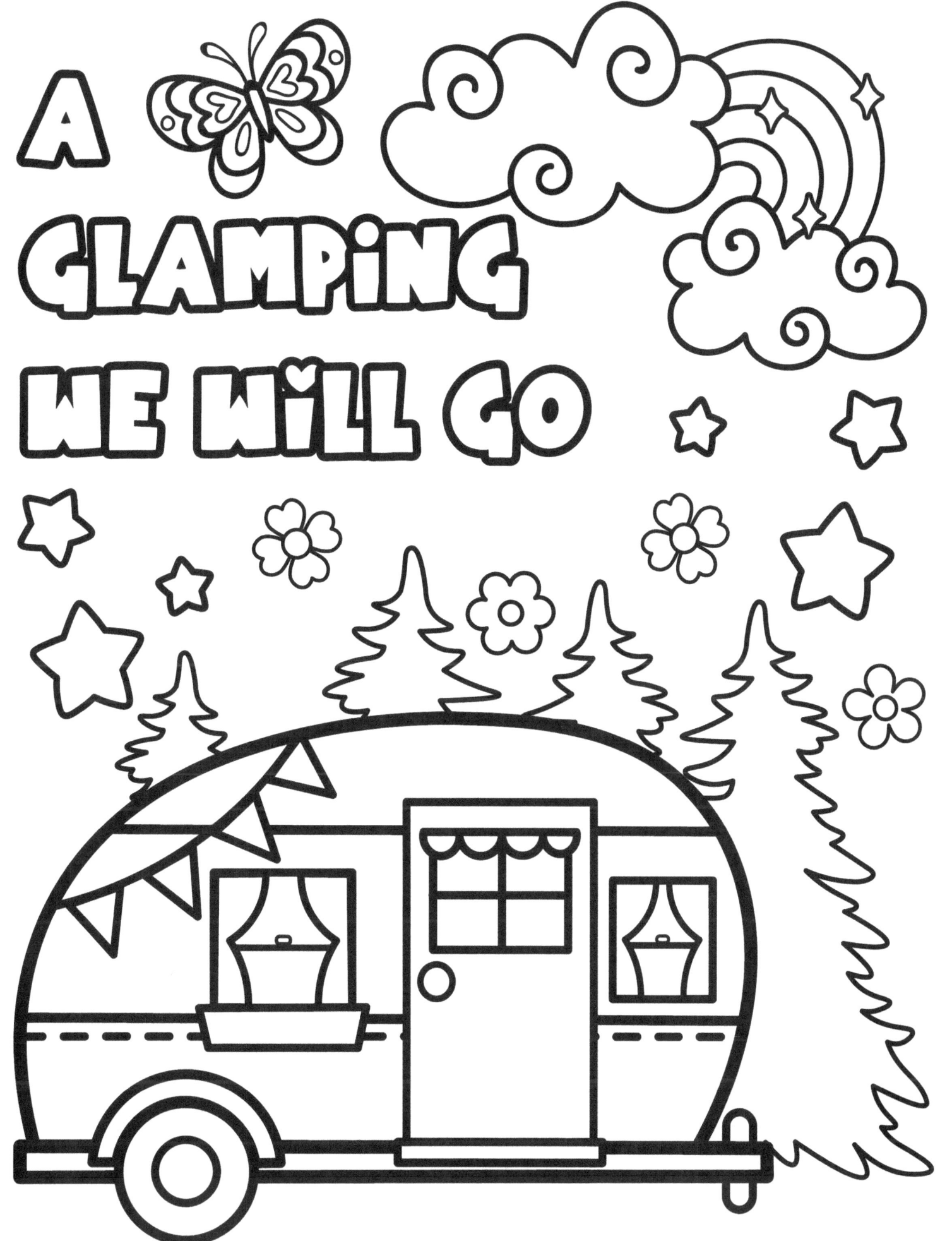

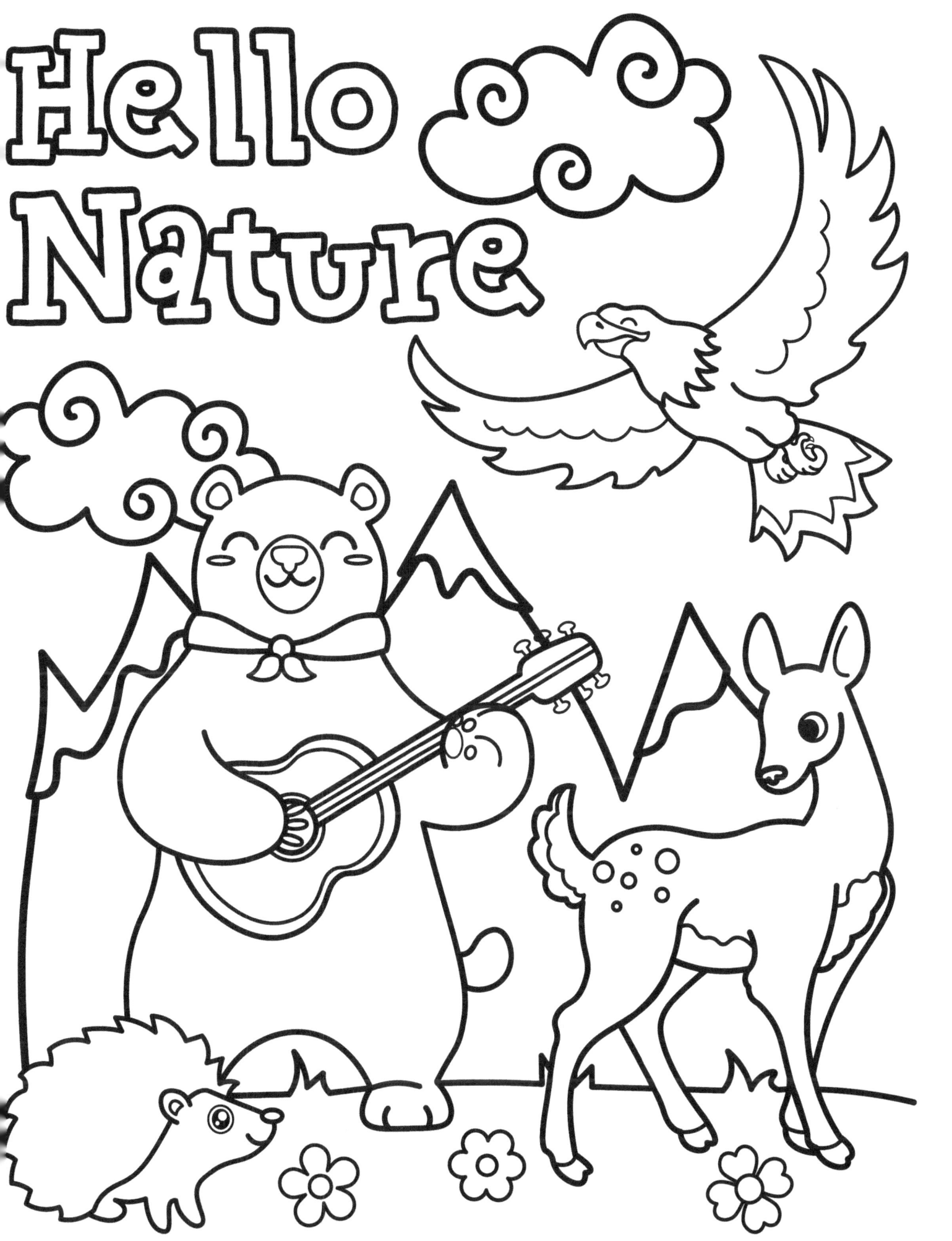

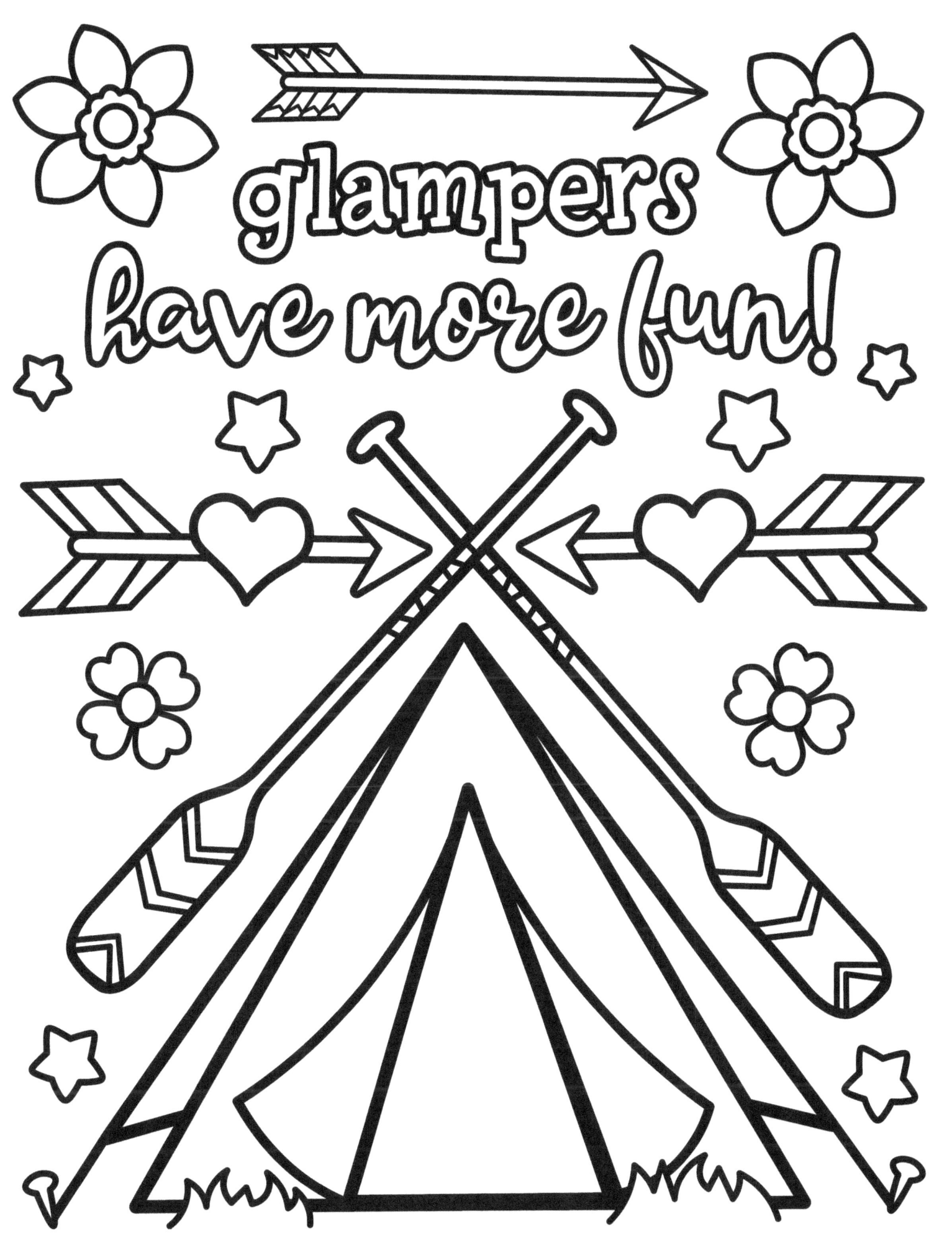

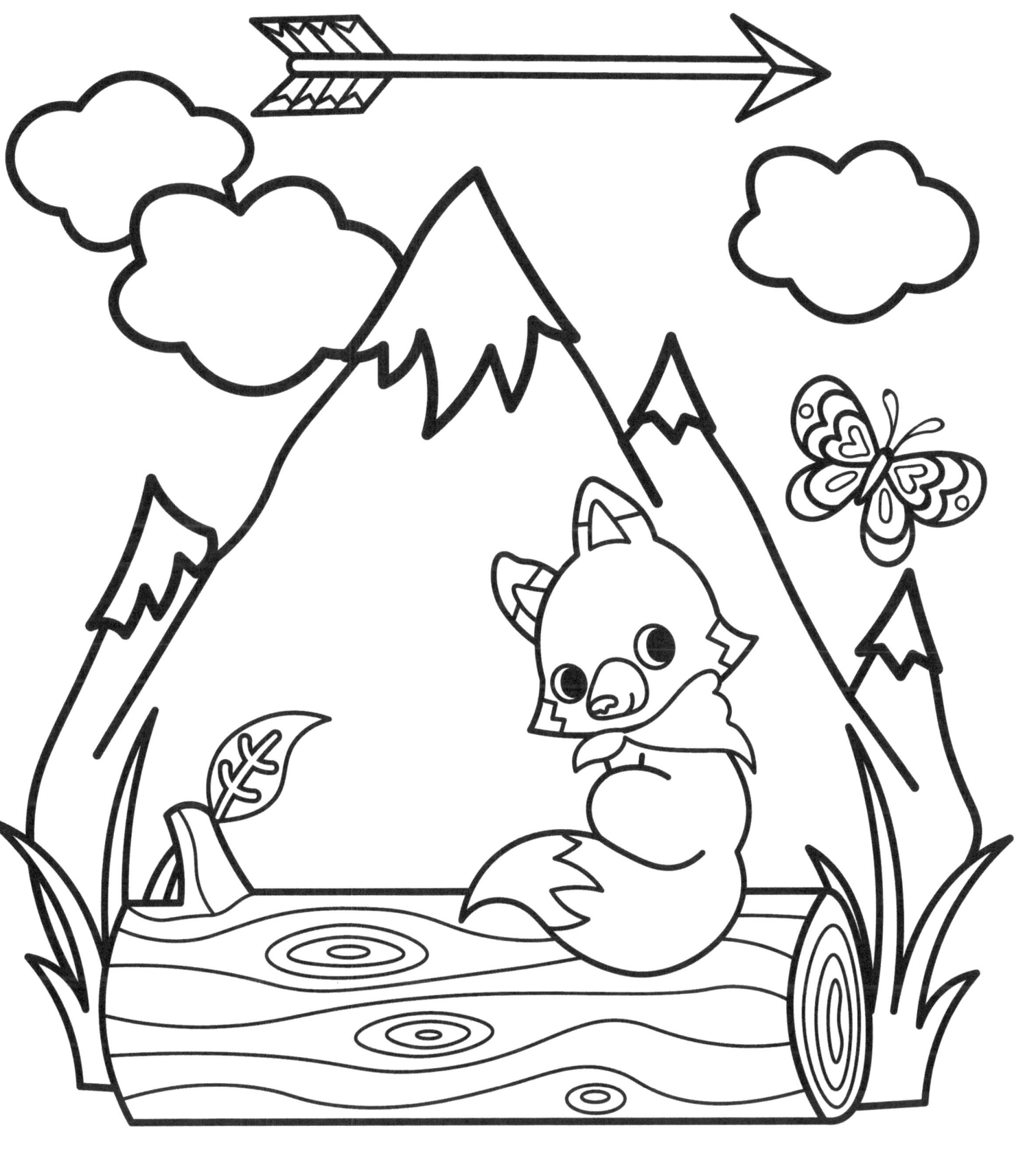

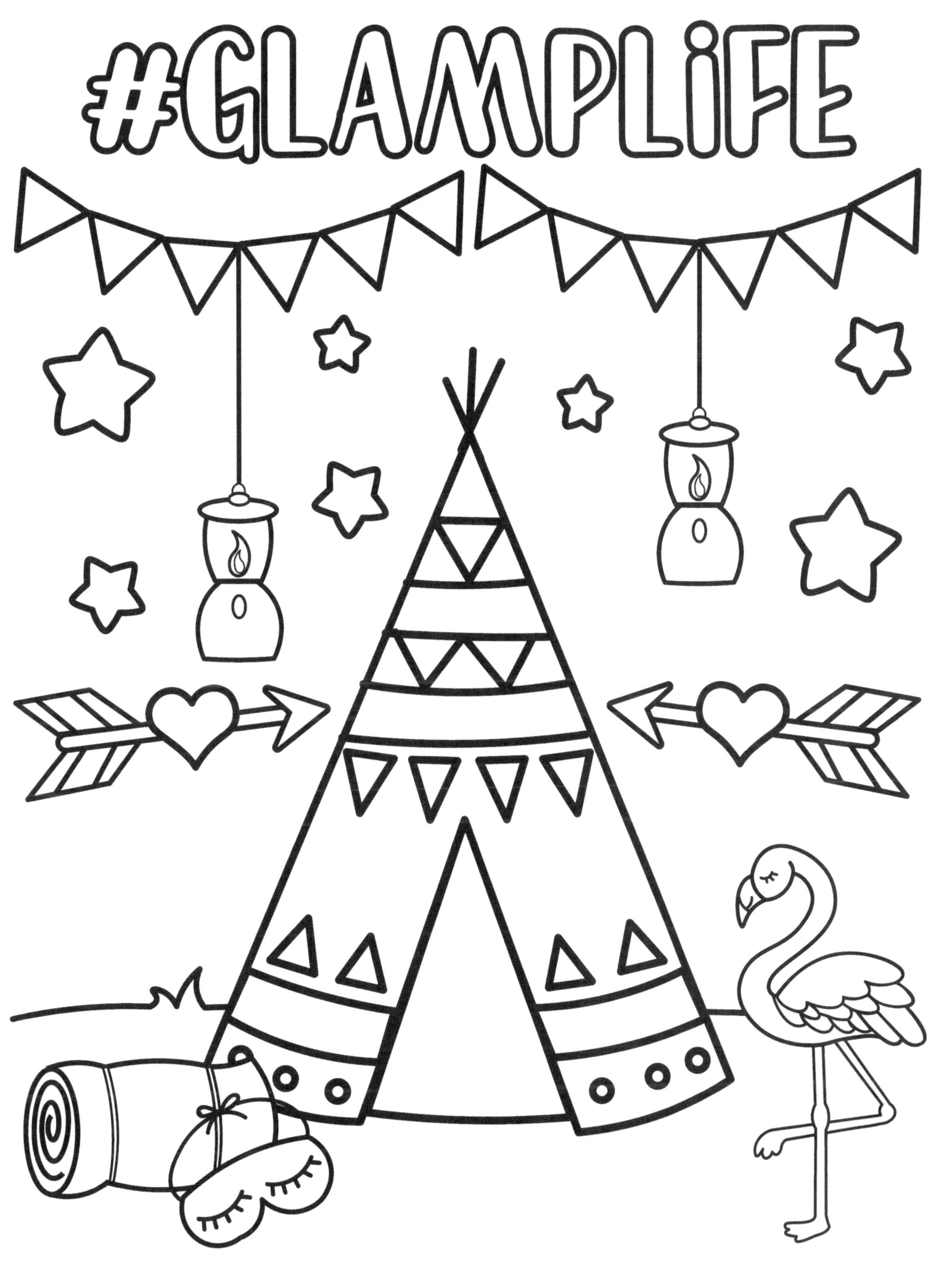

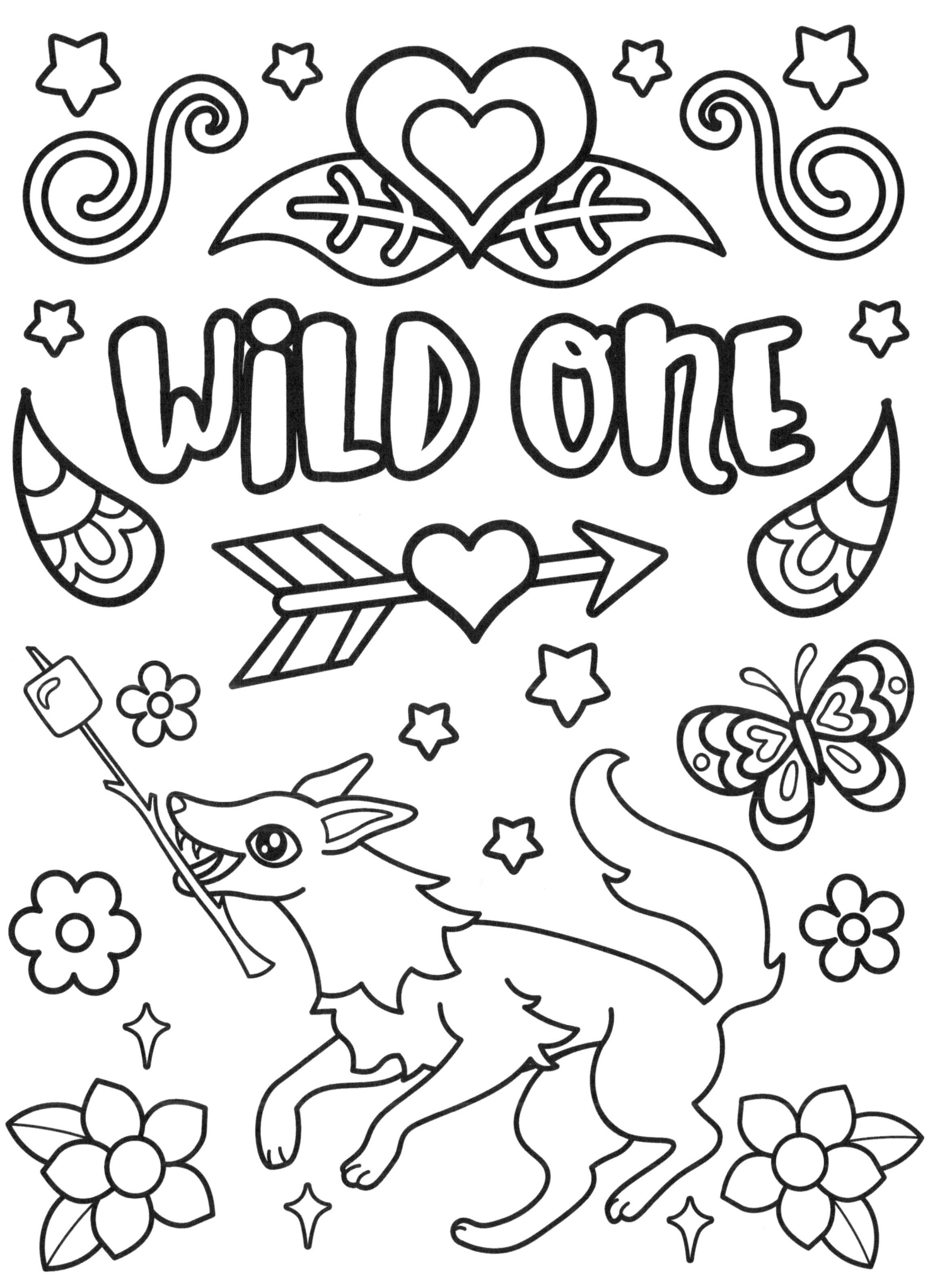

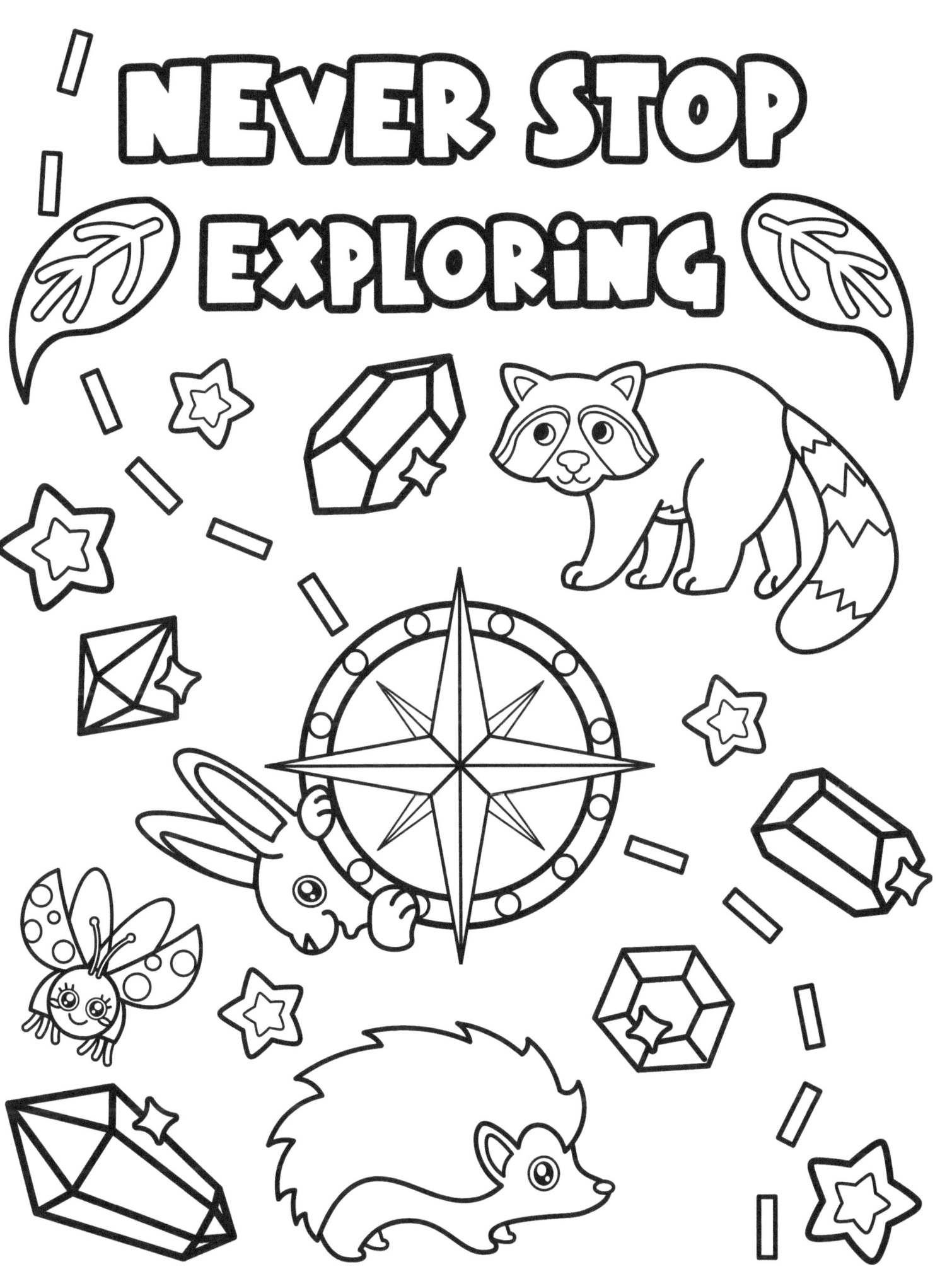

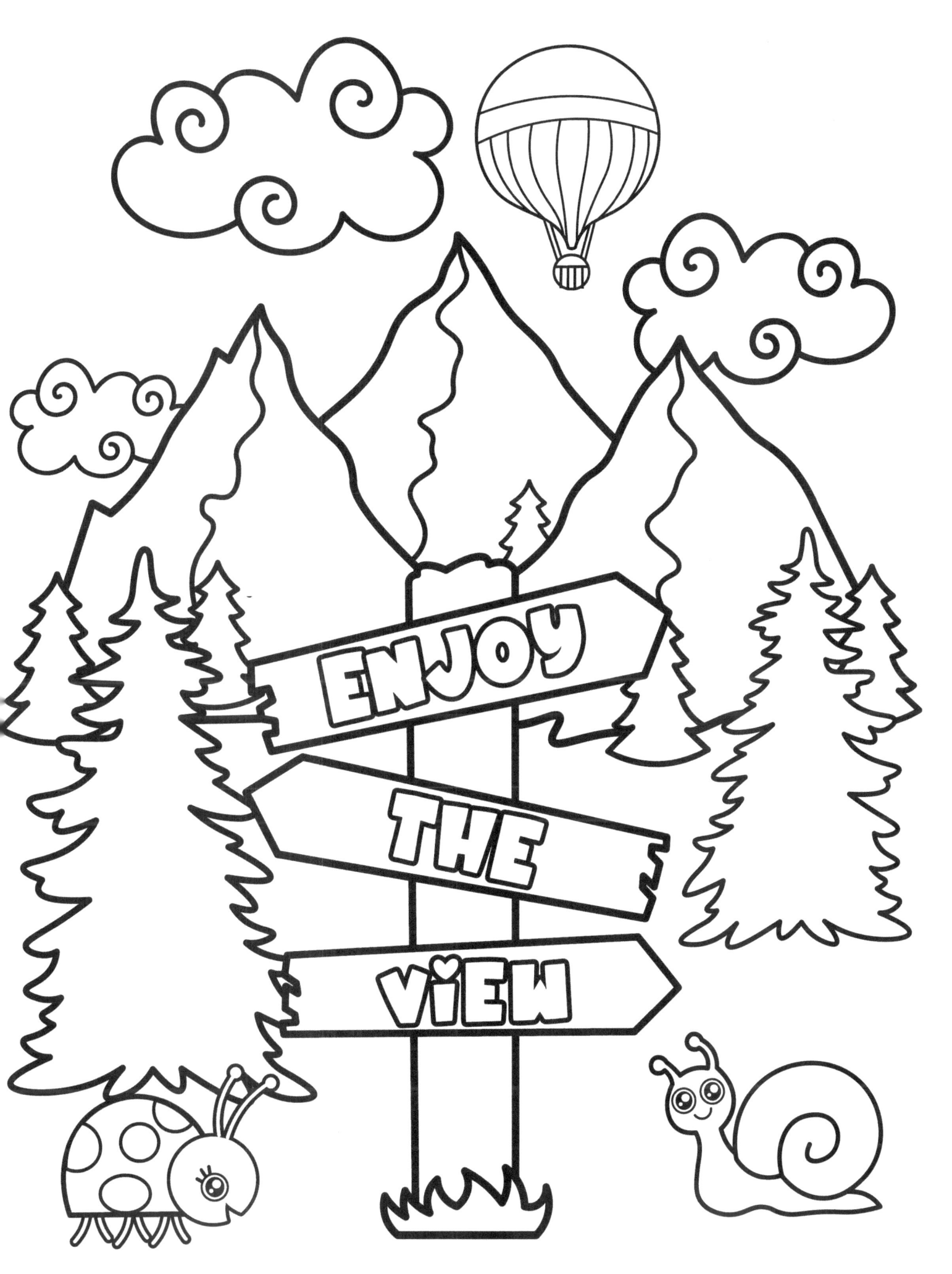

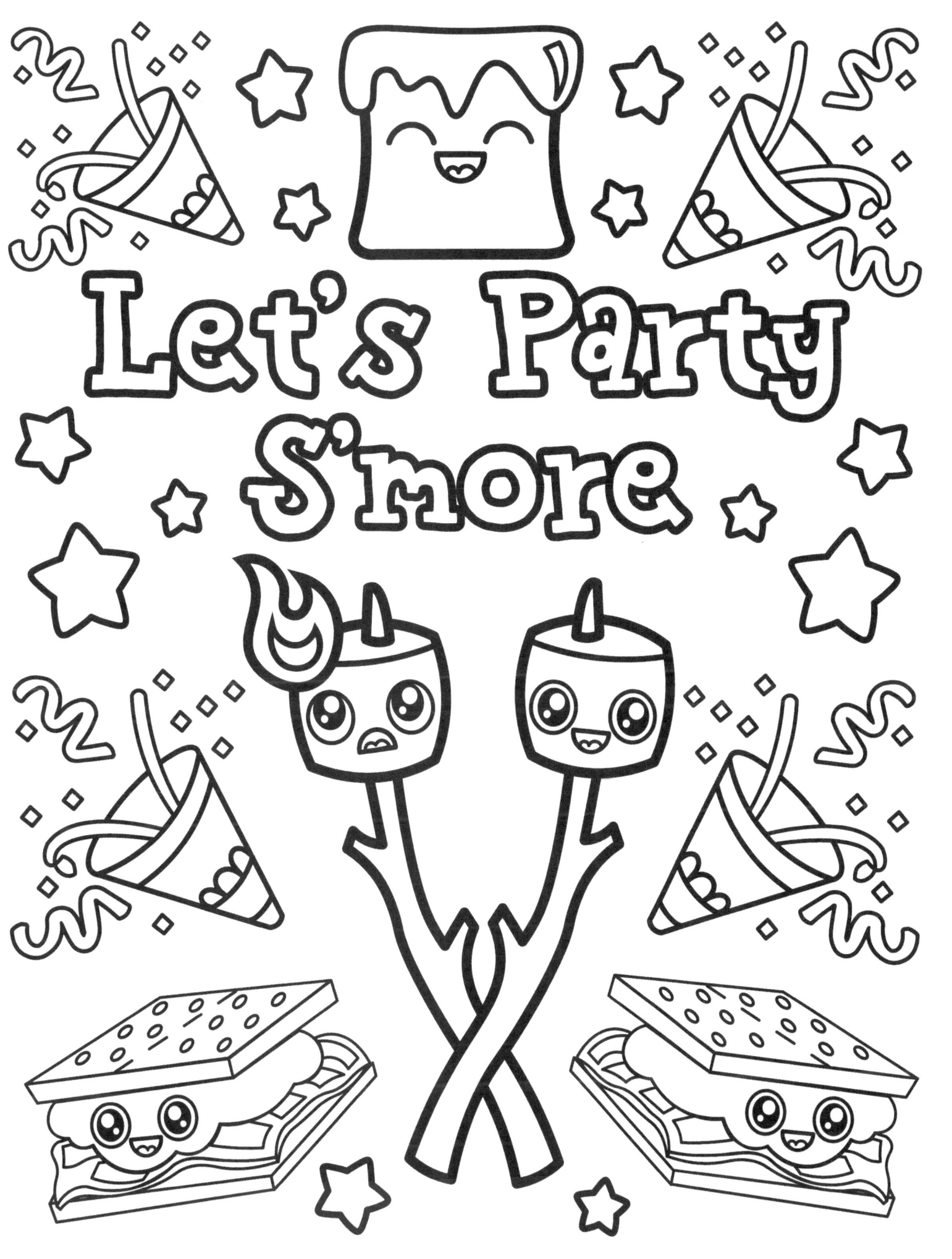

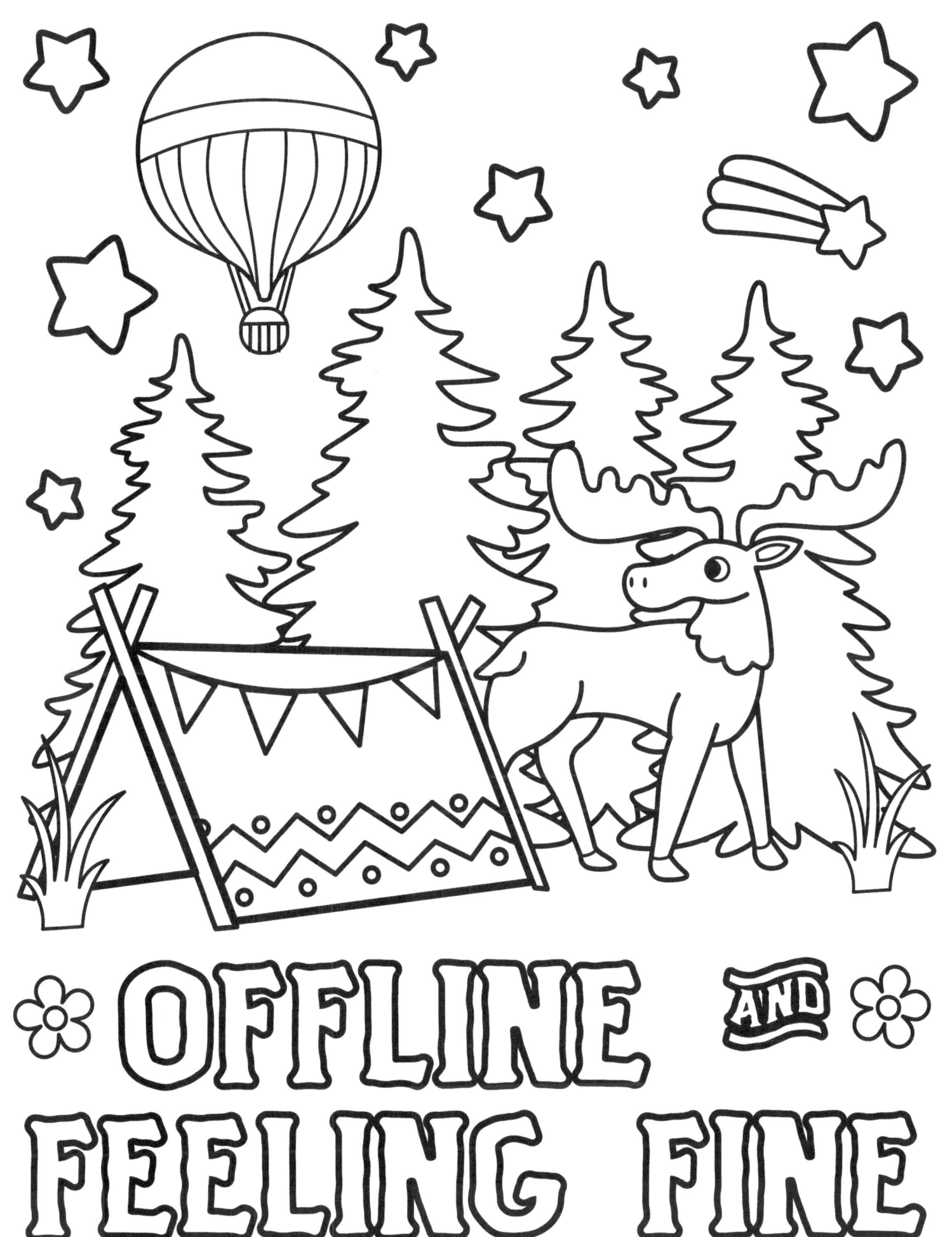

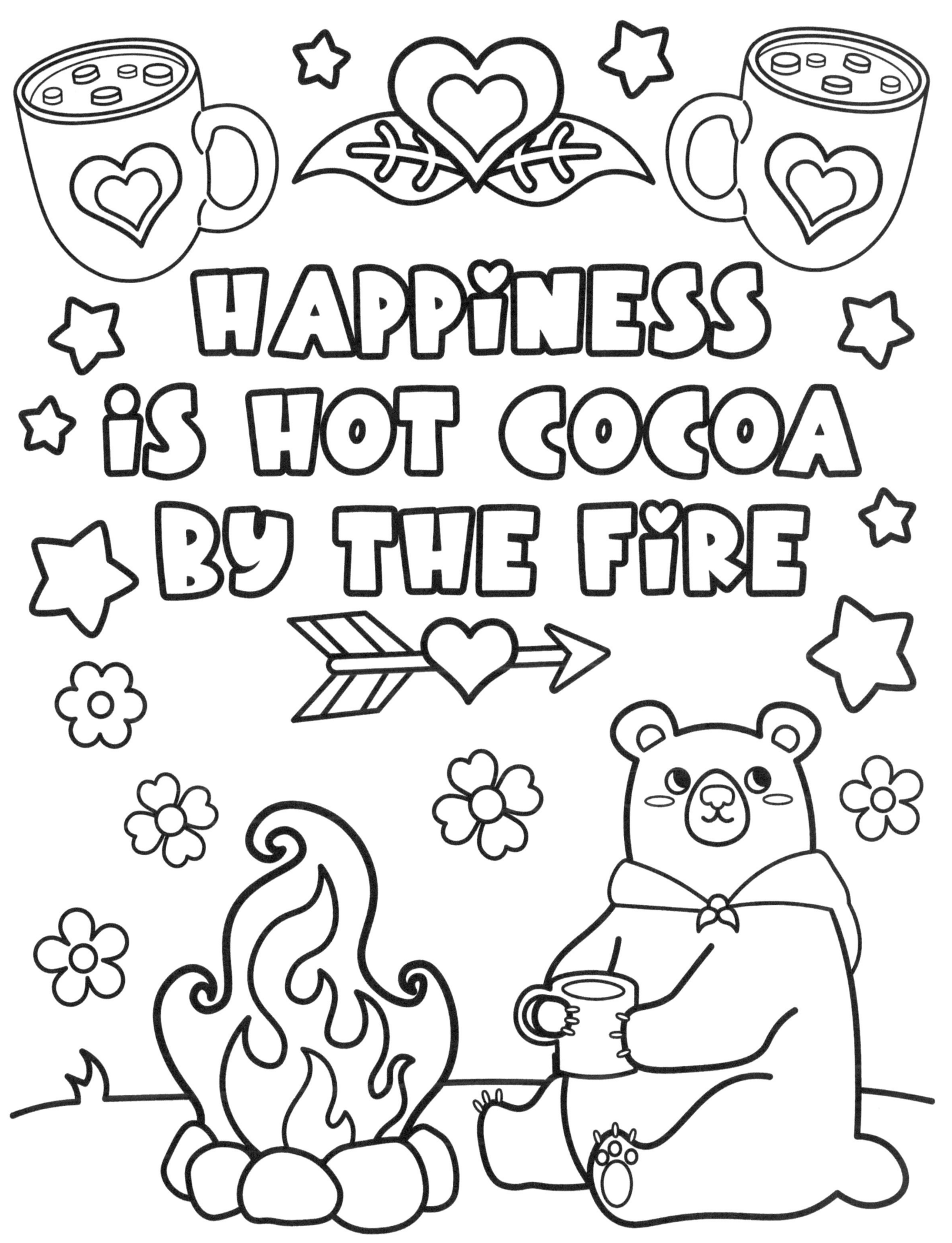

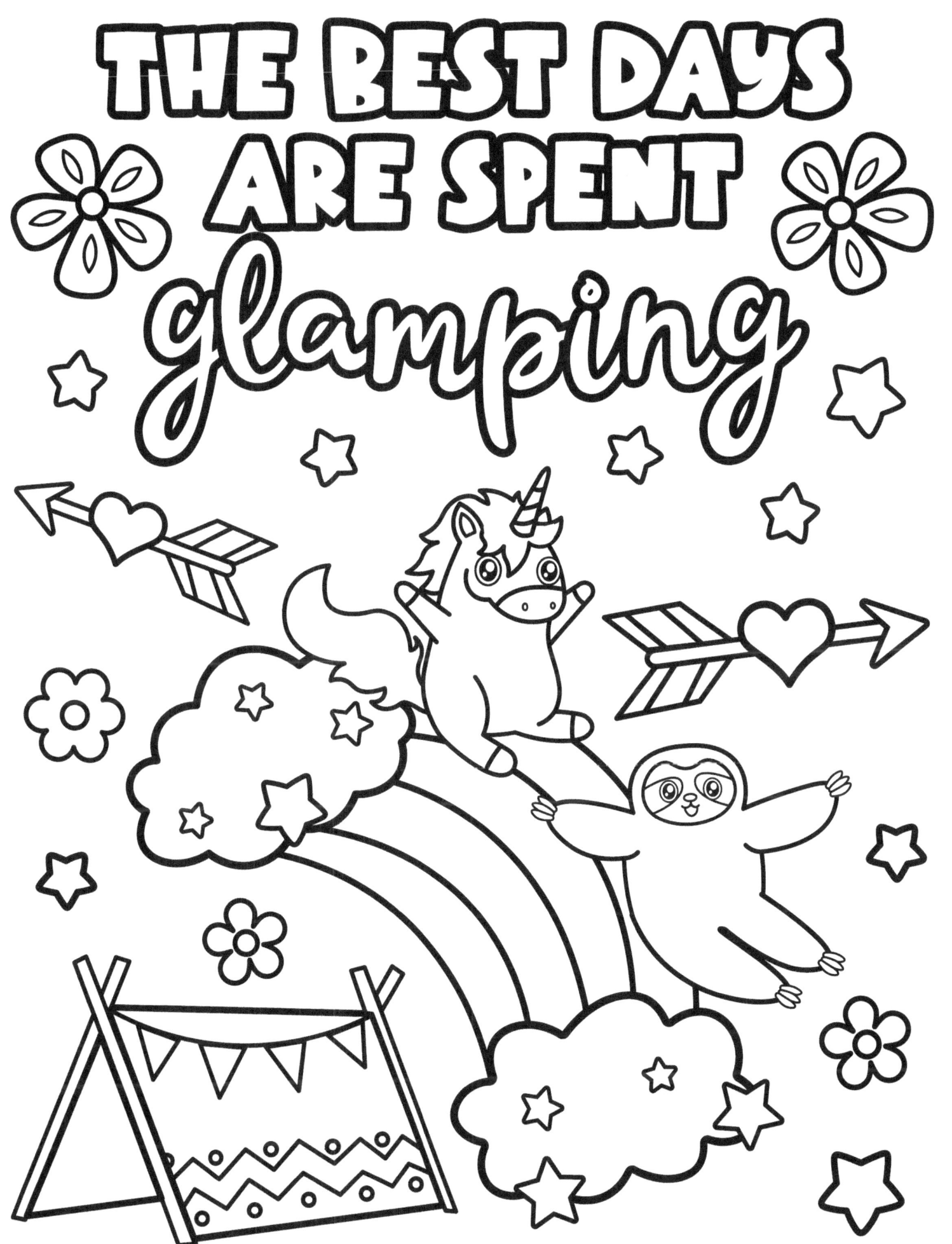

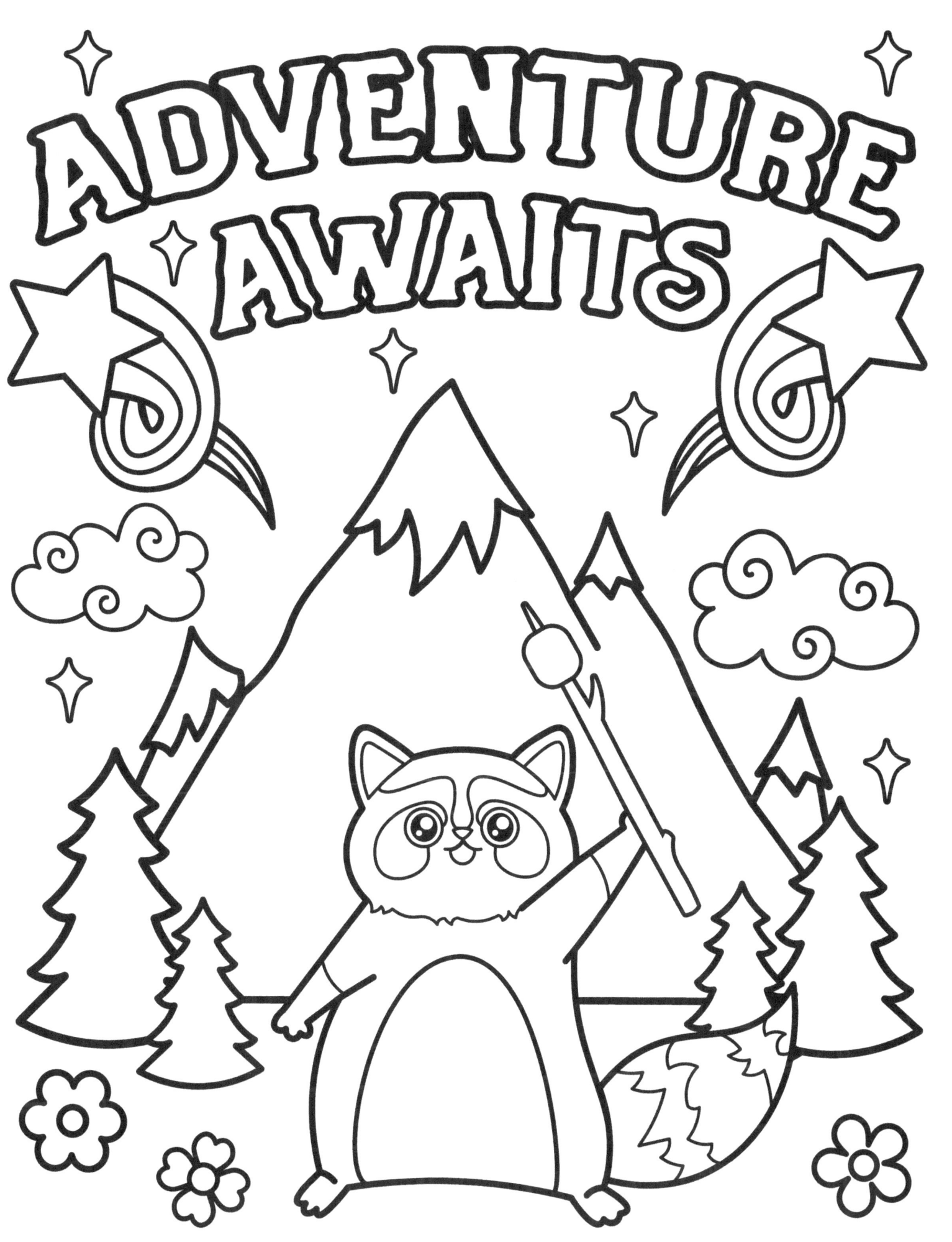

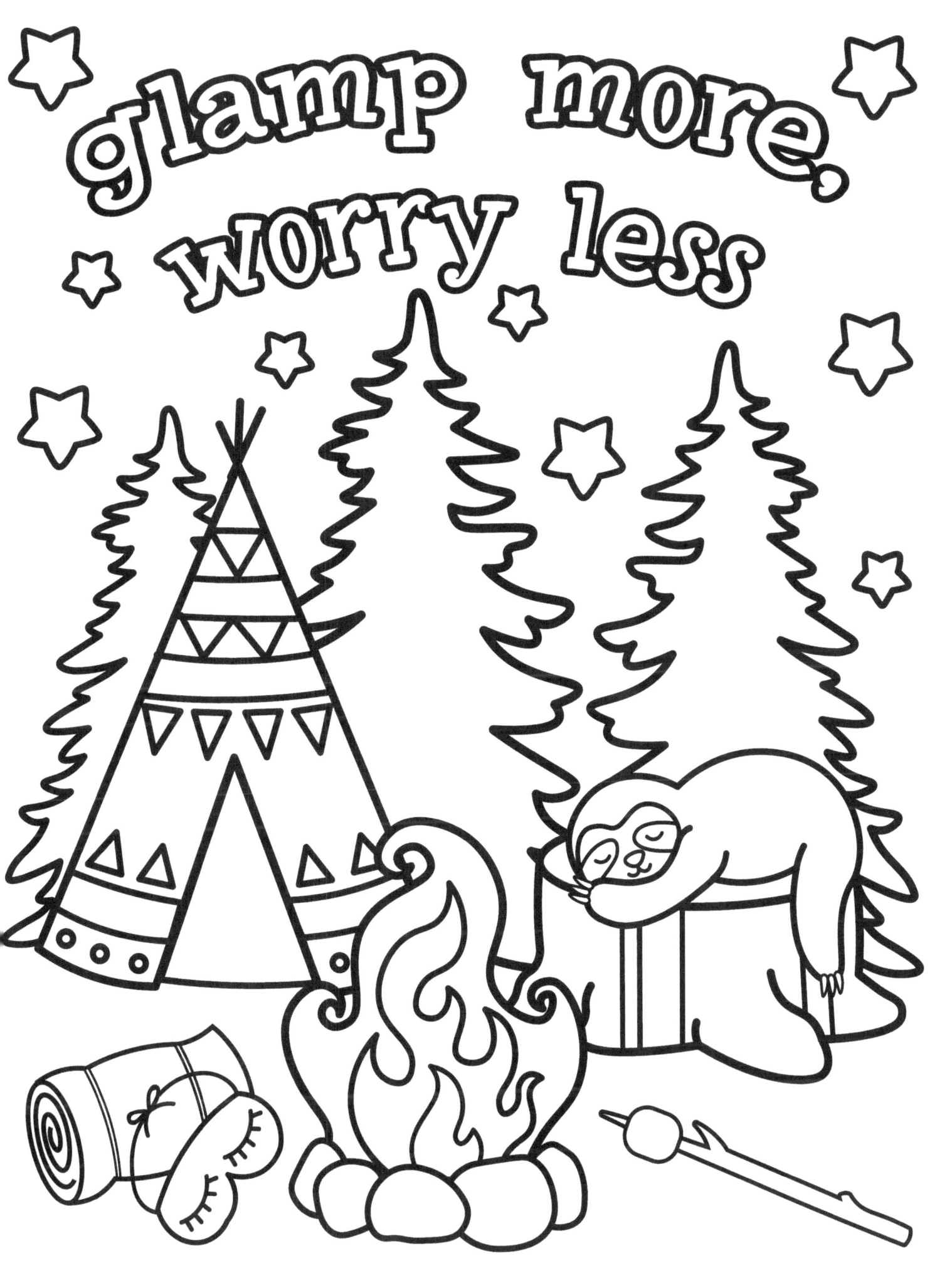

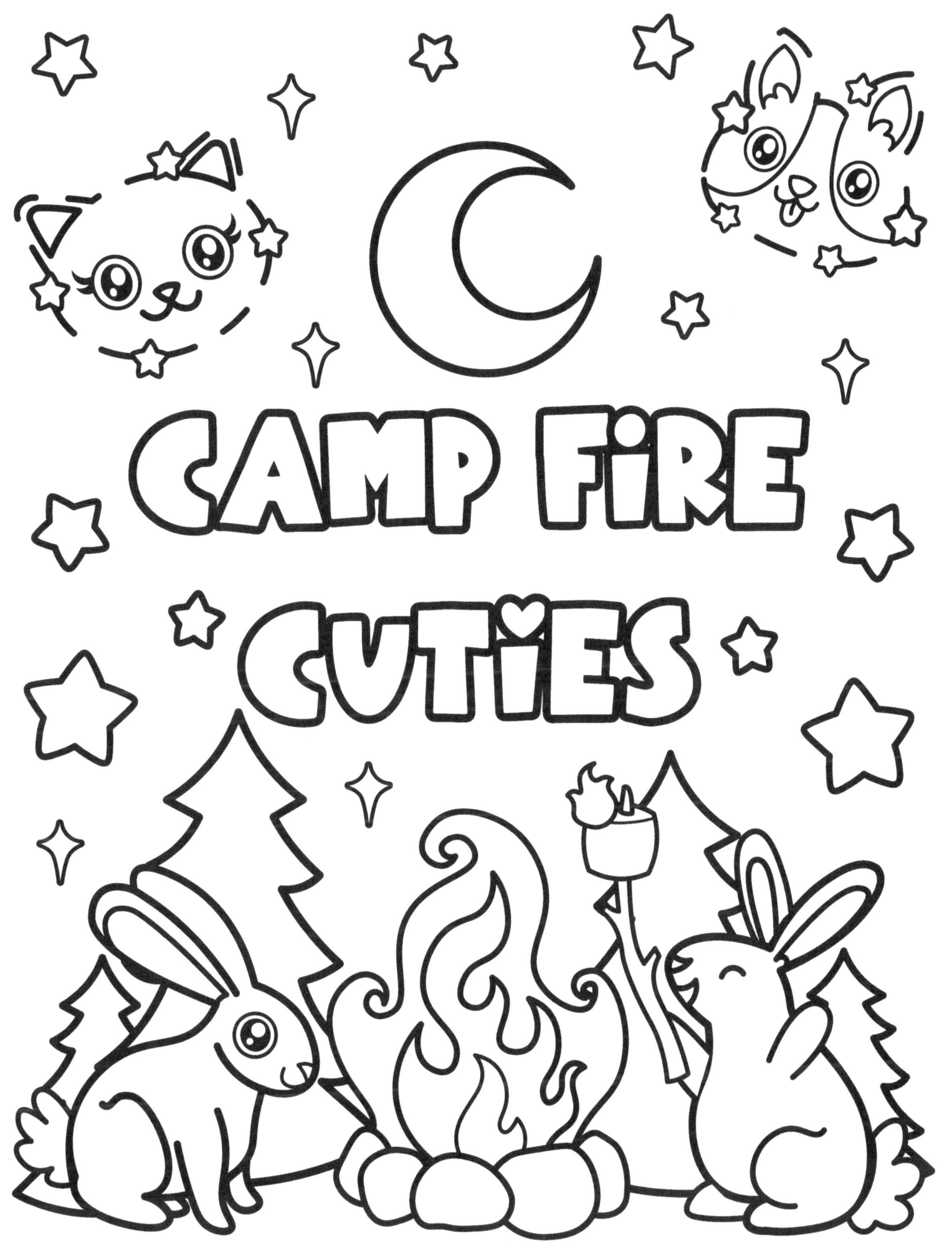

PLEASE, LEAVE US A REVIEW

Thank you for purchasing this Coloring Book. If you enjoyed this book, please leave us a review on Amazon.com

We value your comments and input so we can create better content for our future projects. Nyx Spectrum would love to hear what you think about our books!

Thank you!

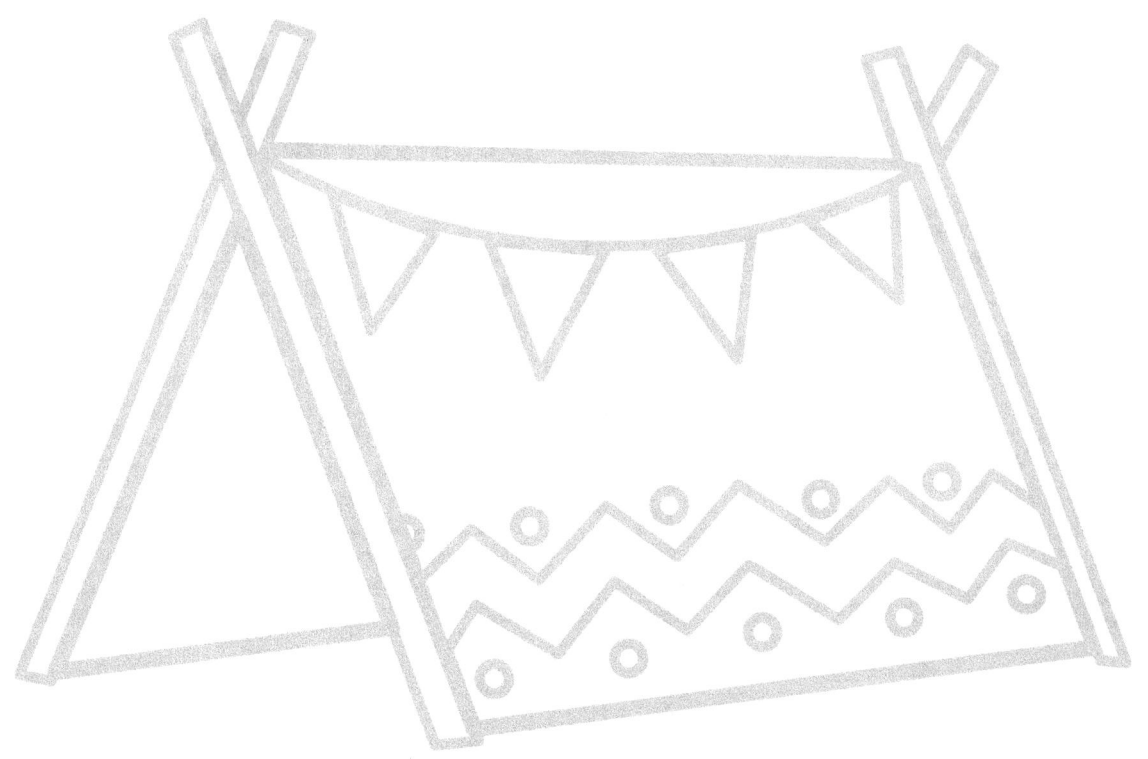

Also by Nyx Spectrum:

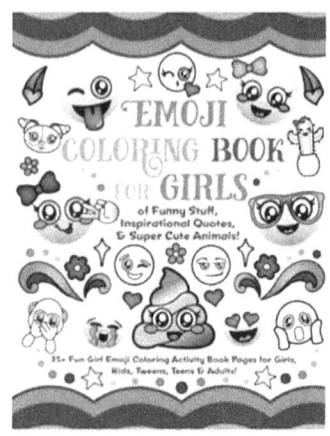 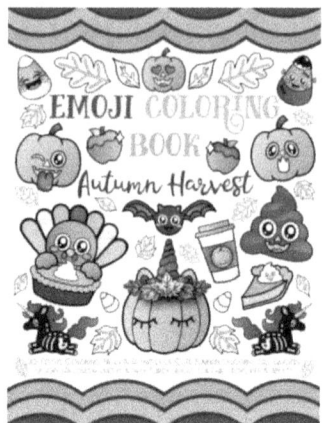 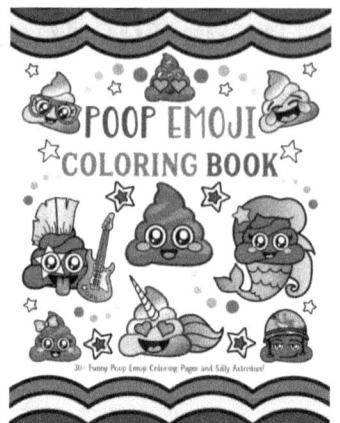 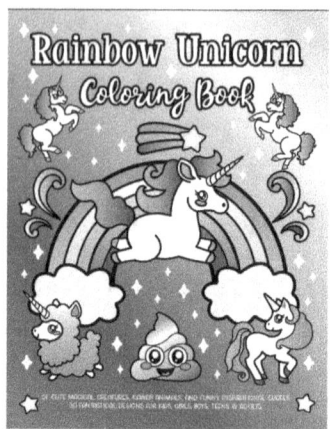

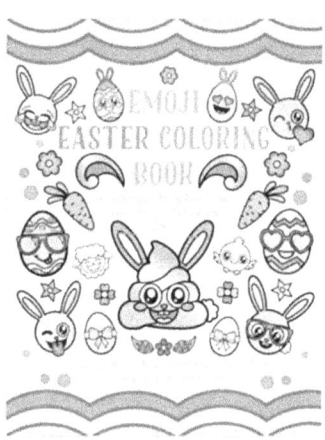 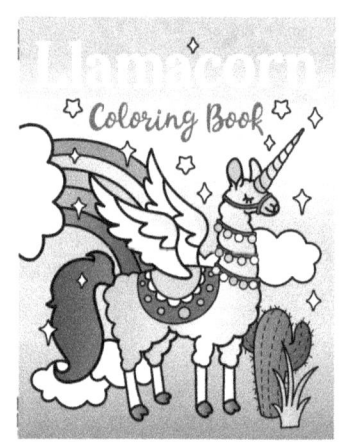 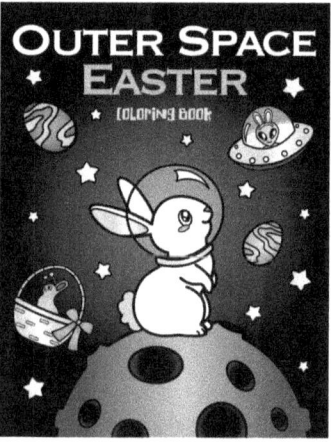 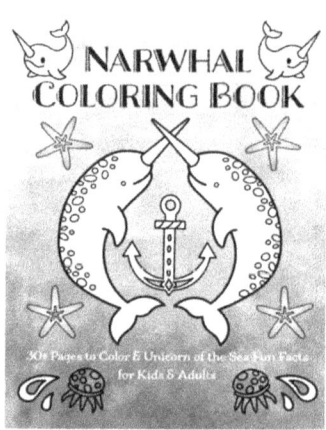

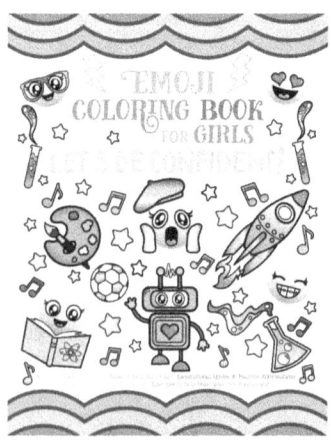 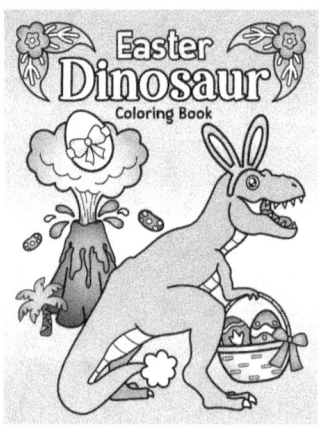 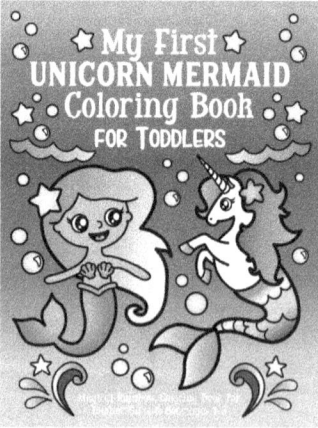 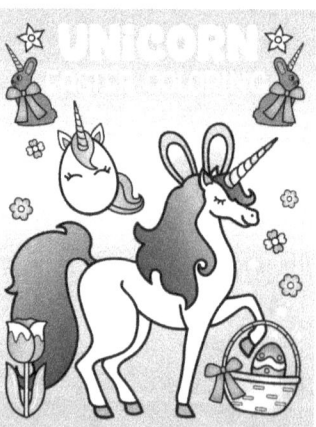

To receive Free exclusive Coloring Pages and future release updates,
please visit us at NyxSpectrum.com and subscribe to our email.
Our books are found only at Amazon.com